THE BOY IN THE BASEMENT

Cataloging-in-Publication data

Angela Lacy McClintock

The Boy in the Basement

ISBN (Paperback) 9798648691070

ISBN (ePub e-book)

ISBN (Hardcover)

First Edition published 2020

Second Edition published 2024

Independently Published

Author Website: www.writeramcclintock.com
Author Email: writeramcclintock@gmail.com

This is a work of fiction. Names, characters, businesses, places, events, locales, and incidents are either the products of the author's imagination or used in a fictitious manner. Any resemblance to actual persons, living or dead, or actual events is purely coincidental.

There are over 320,000 Child Welfare social workers in the United States alone. Despite very little recognition, low wages, and difficult working conditions, these brave soldiers go out into the darkness every day to illuminate the plight of abused children. Thanks to all these brave soldiers for the sacrifices they make every day to protect children. May the good you do be noticed and lauded.

Angela Lacy McClintock

Content Warning
This book contains fictional accounts of child physical abuse, sexual abuse, family violence, and mental illness. Some readers may find this disturbing. Please consider this as you choose this book.

The Boy in the Basement

McClintock

1

Prologue

The boy sat cross-legged on the cement floor; his bare feet black. Craning his neck upward, he peered longingly at the small basement window and stretched out thin arms to soak up the last vestige of warmth the light had to offer. From the window, a rectangular patch of pink sky signaled the last gasp of an autumn day.

Unsure of how long the basement had been his prison, the nine-year-old remembered few clues. It had been the end of summer when momma locked him in, and his Iron Man pajamas had been new and clean. The ragged hem of his PJs and the faded superhero on his chest told him that none of that was true anymore.

The child guessed it must be Halloween because she came down and got the skeleton off the storeroom shelf. On Halloween, she always placed the life-size bony man on the porch rocker next to that smoking ice stuff.

Was it only this morning when he saw her? She had not spoken to him, barely noticed him. Of course, he made himself as small as possible, pretending to be asleep on the cement floor and watching her behind lidded eyes. She giggled while retrieving the plastic bones, causing him to flinch in response.

Uncertainty pricked at his skin like the bites of tiny ants. She had seemed happy. He almost called out to her but stopped short when he remembered the last time. Small, dirty hands instinctively rubbed his cheek, mentally feeling the sting of her nails again as they touched the scabbed-over scars. In rushed the familiar fear, squeezing his chest, his breath escaping in short gasps.

He willed himself invisible as the staccato click of her heels echoed back up the stairs. When the door slammed, and the clink of the bolt sounded, he let the silence fall around him and bring him peace.

The basement used to be so scary. He remembered the fear, the confusion, and the pain as his cries to her were met with a slap or ignored. Back then, he thought he would surely die alone and in the dark. But that didn't happen. Every night, he fell asleep wondering if things would be better in the morning. But the thoughts of rescue had vanished long ago.

Now, the silence felt safe. Surrounded by familiarity, he drew comfort in the sour, earthy smell and the safety of his concrete cage.

While he pondered, darkness crept stealthily into the basement, its frigid fingertips creating shadows in every corner. He watched as the night came slowly into his world inch by inch until he felt its icy breath on his arms and shivered. There had been no food today. That was the one downfall of being forgotten. But of all the evils, hunger was the lesser one. He had learned to eat what he could find, often sneaking things out of the deep freezer. As long as the order of things was not disturbed, she wouldn't find out and punish him.

The boy tried to open the heavy lid quietly, grimacing for the tell-tale squeak of an un-oiled hinge. It did not budge. Confused, he slid his hand beneath the handle, wrapping his small fingers around something cold and hard. Slowly, confusion turned to anxiety. When had she locked the freezer? She must have noticed the hot dogs he had stolen the night before and put the lock on while he slept.

He shook his head, dizzy from hunger. Accepting that there would be no food tonight, he placed his tiny hands on the water heater, absorbing the cast-off heat. Then, making a soft place out of old newspapers, he drew his legs up into his chest and fell into an uneasy sleep.

2

Jennifer

"Hey, folks! Guess what? It's another muggy Autumn day in Mobile, Alabama! If you're new to the area, I have some bad news for you. Get used to it. What the brochure didn't tell you was that winter in Mobile starts and ends in February!"

Jennifer Riley grimaced as the sports news announcer repeated the same tired old joke. Yet, his words touched on the truth. As a coastal city in the South, Mobile winters were mild, and, Yes, often muggy when the air sauntered in from the Gulf of Mexico. But she had to admit that warm winters sure beat ice and snow. Perhaps that explained why so many snowbirds–those retired folks from New York, Chicago, and Detroit– loved to spend the winter here.

It was Halloween. For most of the world above the Mason-Dixon line, the holiday offered cool weather activities: bonfires, hayrides, and parties for kids and some adults who still felt like kids. No one's building a bonfire in Mobile. Jennifer noticed the temperature had been seventy-five degrees that morning when she left her apartment and was forecasted to climb to a soupy eighty-five by the afternoon. She had dressed accordingly in loose-fitting linen slacks and a sleeveless silk blouse. The vibrant jade set off her pale grey eyes and long auburn hair, now pulled back into a loose French braid.

Whispering a brief prayer of thanks for the office air-conditioner, she leaned back in her chair as she listened to the ESPN app on her cell. Sipping the mocha latte, Jennifer closed her eyes in an effort to ignore the stacks of loose papers, colored folders, and spreadsheets covering the surface of her desk.

At the Department of Human Resources, Child Protective Services (known as CPS) Jennifer investigated child abuse cases. While some social workers found ways to escape the high-pressure unit after only a few months, she loved the fast-paced emergencies and split-second decision-making that came to be expected of a CPS investigator. A decade later, after resisting the promotion offer of her superiors for years, she finally agreed to supervise when the SAB (Severe Abuse Unit) came open. The SAB handled the most serious injuries inflicted upon children, including death. Jennifer, excited about the challenge, felt she could bring her experience to the unit as a supervisor.

Because of the unrelenting pace that attracted her to the unit, Jennifer liked to come in early, drink her coffee, and organize herself for the day ahead. That morning, she set her cell to the sports radio network and listened as fellow Bama fans blew up the station with their on-air brags about how badly the Crimson Tide had defeated the Tennessee Volunteers. Jennifer smiled to herself and spoke aloud to the radio, "What did you expect, people? The Vols haven't had a decent year since Phil Fulmer."

The door opened slightly, and she heard a deep baritone. "Jennifer, got a minute?"

Startled, she jumped slightly in her chair and turned off the radio. Smiling widely, she answered, "Hey, Michael, what's up?"

"Sorry to bother you," said the light-skinned African American. "Especially during your victory dance," he teased.

Michael had only been with the unit for a year but had already shown initiative and an analytical mind. Jennifer saw the potential immediately when he had interviewed for the job.

Jennifer rolled her eyes. "Don't be that jealous Auburn fan, Michael. Have patience; we will also beat you in a few weeks."

"All I can say to that is War Eagle." he grinned.

"You poor deluded soul," she chuckled. "How can I help you?"

"I just wondered if I could pick your brain?"

"Sure! What little there is to pick before I finish my coffee."

"Real quick. Got allegations that mom abused prescription drugs. She did a pee test, but when I got her screen back, she tested positive for amphetamines. She swore the only prescription she took was for Lortab after a root canal."

"Lortabs are opiates, not amphetamines."

"Yes, I know," he grinned. "Herein lies my dilemma. She didn't test positive for opiates at all."

"Okay. What does that tell you?" Jennifer kept prodding.

"That the amphetamines could be illegal, or the drug lab made a mistake."

"I like that you didn't just jump to the conclusion that mom was dirty. You will learn in this unit that my favorite motto is Dig Deeper! In other words, check it out further. Tell her what you found and give her a chance to explain it. If she continues to deny using amphetamines, get a hair follicle test, and we will see what that shows. The kids are with grandmother right now anyway, right?"

"Right,

"Cool. Talk to mom, set up the second test, and then transfer this case to family preservation. They can follow up and offer supervision and monitoring. I need you clear today. You're up first for an emergency."

"Will do, boss. Anything in yet?"

"I have a few red files on my desk from the overnight unit. I am getting ready to go over them now. If something flags an emergency, I will buzz you."

After Michael left her office, Jennifer looked longingly at her phone, wanting to hear the rest of the sports program. Instead, she finished her coffee and started organizing her desk into two piles: New cases to be assigned and those that required her review and approval to close.

The review pile, with six completed cases, stood taller than the intake pile of two cases. Jennifer knew there would be no going home tonight if she did not close those out. On the last day of the month, in CPS jargon, all cases from the past 60 days had to be cleared off the system by midnight. The state allotted only 60 days to investigate, dictate, and submit a case for closure. The last day of the month often turned into a late night as workers scrambled to get their notes and dispositions into the system.

However, the two red intake folders indicated a significant child safety issue. Jennifer decided to assess the emergent nature of the intakes to determine if either of them warranted an immediate victim response. Then she would tackle the higher pile.

The first red folder held one sheet of paper, signifying that the family had no prior abuse or neglect complaints.

"Hmmm. One-year-old with a spiral fracture of unknown origin. Brought into Providence this morning by a babysitter." Jennifer often read the intakes aloud to help her process the information.

She found that by hearing the narrative, a clear analytical picture formed in her mind, helping her assess danger. Technically, this particular intake did not rise to the level of immediate danger due to a host of unknown factors. However, due to the vulnerability of the child's age and the access of the alleged perpetrators, it would be wise to send someone to check it out today.

She called Kim Stillwell to her office. Kim, a veteran of the CPS program, had transferred the previous week into SAB. Her former supervisor in the sexual abuse unit highly recommended her. Jennifer was curious to see the investigator's reaction to being sent out immediately on a technical non-emergency, knowing she probably had multiple reports to clear up.

"Yes, ma'am," the long-legged blonde entered Jennifer's office. Short curls framed her round face, lending her an air of innocence. Her southern drawl was even more pronounced than most in the office, so the one-syllable word lasted for two.

"Kim, I need you to go out on an immediate response case." She handed over the folder. "It's a toddler with a broken arm at Providence. It may be an honest accident, but we just don't know."

"Good Lord! I mean, I guess we don't want to jump to conclusions, but kids that age don't usually just break their bones. In my wound identification class, Doc Silver said their bones are more pliable at that age."

She glanced again at the intake and then added, "I'll go right now and let you know if there's anything to this."

"Good deal. I will cross you off the list to get a case today so you can work on this one."

"Thanks, but if things get all crazy-cat around here and you need me to take another, just holler."

Jennifer liked the drive she saw in Kim. She would fit in well with this unit.

The other red folder bulged with papers. Pulling it closer, Jennifer began reading the second emergency intake, which was far more substantial. A six-month-old on life support with suspicion of traumatic brain injury. As she read the information from the hospital, her stomach tightened. This would not end well.

Jennifer closed her eyes and spent several minutes processing the information she had read. When she opened her eyes, she dialed an extension.

Voicemail notified her that Daniel Bradshaw was unable to take her call.

"Daniel, I need you to come to my office as soon as you get this. I need you to take a bad one," she said into the receiver.

While she waited for him, she decided to delve into the case history to gain a better understanding of the family dynamic.

Thirty minutes later, after completing her review, she redialed Daniel's extension. This time he answered on the first ring.

"Daniel Bradshaw."

"Daniel," Jennifer scolded mildly. "Do you not listen to your voicemails, or is it just me you ignore?"

"Jenn, why would I ever ignore you?"

She ignored the banter and his infuriating insistence on giving her a nickname. "Daniel, I need you to come to my office now. We have a high-profile case."

"On my way."

A few minutes later, he entered her office and sat facing her desk. "Yes, ma'am?"

Living in the South, the expected practice of using the terms sir and ma'am prevailed, but Daniel was 42 years old, ten years her senior, so it felt strange when he called her ma'am.

"Daniel, I have a serious emergency for you."

"No problem, but I thought Michael was up first today?"

"He is. But I want you. Michael is running down some leads on another case, and frankly, I want him to get some more experience before tackling something like this. I need your expertise."

"Yeah, sure, use the flattery when you want something." His lips turned up in a brief smile. "Whatcha got?"

Daniel smiled and wiped away the lock of hair that hung in his eyes. He was already graying, with streaks of salt and pepper in his hair, but his face was so youthful that most people didn't believe he was 42. His black/brown eyes were extremely intense. They could be beautiful and peaceful when he was calm but fiery and ice-cold when he was "in the zone." His skin was beautiful– the color of café au lait– a rich, creamy hue that gave him that 'perpetual tan' look coveted on the Gulf Coast.

Jennifer began. "I got a six-month-old baby on a ventilator in the USA. Could be shaken baby, could be natural, could be something else. But the kicker is that Mom's history reads like a "lifetime movie.""

Daniel's smile faded as he took out his notebook. "So, I am guessing that mom was in the system?"

"Foster care since the age of 14."

"Geez. That's never a good sign for lifelong stability." Daniel clicked his pen and added, "I'm ready; fill me in."

Jennifer took out her own notes and began reading her shorthand account of the past eleven years. "Betty Jo Ossie goes by BJ, so it might be good to remember when trying to establish rapport."

"BJ. Got it."

"Entered foster care at 14, as I said, after her mother died of an overdose of heroin. Because of her age, she went into Miracle House.

"I'm not familiar with that one.," he frowned slightly.

"It's a small group home for teen girls in Bon Secour. Families can place their teens there; DHR doesn't often get a spot."

Daniel nodded. "Learn something new every day."

When he cocked his head like a curious puppy, Jenifer almost laughed. Daniel saw her look of amusement and quickly returned his focus. "Oh, um, I was just processing what you said. Sorry, please continue."

"No need to apologize; I want you to break in if you need clarification. I know I am rattling this off pretty quickly."

Smiling, he said, "I'm caught up now."

"Right," she resumed. "Six months after being placed at Miracle House, she became pregnant. She claimed that one of the night residential staff raped her. However, as no one witnessed it, she was branded a liar and kicked out of the program."

Daniel snorted. "Of course, no one witnessed it. These girls are on psychotropic meds and/or sleeping meds. I have seen this type of residential abuse before. Poor girl."

Jennifer agreed. "Even in the most structured environments, there are people who will take advantage of a vulnerable kid. I mean, who listens to them? When it's their words against a trusted staff member." She let her voice trail off.

"Congregate care is not the panacea for the ills of foster care," he mused.

"Agreed, but let's move on. I know that's a hill we can't climb today." Jennifer glanced at her notes. "She was moved to a residential facility after the Miracle House. That's where she gave birth."

"The baby?" asked Daniel, writing furiously as his supervisor talked.

"That child went into the system and was adopted by his foster parents."

"Really? Her rights were terminated. Was there any effort of re-unification?"

"Not that I can tell. Her story never wavered about the rape, but because of her already seductive behaviors, nobody believed her. She withdrew even more into herself and started using drugs."

Daniel just listened and nodded.

Jennifer continued. "For the next few years, BJ went in and out of group homes and institutions, making progress and then self-destructing."

"Wow. Poor Kid."

"Then, inexplicably, something changed. She was placed with a very experienced, older foster couple who refused to allow BJ to push them away. After a few really tough years, where they hung on by teeth and toenails, she settled down. She completed her outpatient program and, with the support of her foster parents, engaged in community volunteer projects. Daniel, she even completed her GED and was accepted in the CNA program at Bishop State."

Daniel interjected. "I'm sensing a 'but coming."

Jennifer nodded. "And you would be right. After Bishop State, she started working in a nursing home where she met and hooked up with Brian McArthur, an orderly. They moved in together, and less than a year later, Jason, her son, was born."

"What happened?" mused Daniel.

"After Jason was born, the Department received several reports of Domestic Violence. Specifically, reports that Brian was beating BJ. But like most DV cases, because BJ refused to press charges, nothing could be proven."

"She probably had no idea how to survive and care for Jason. So, she took the abuse."

Jennifer agreed. "I know we have seen that so many times. But in BJ's case, things changed when we started getting reports of unexplained bruises on Jason. When Brian began to take out his anger on her son, BJ admitted that her boyfriend was using meth and beating them both."

"She actually got out of the situation?" Daniel was listening intently.

"Family Preservation got involved and assigned a social worker to BJ. The social worker helped BJ and Jason find placement at Penelope House while the police served a Protection from Abuse order on Brian. The worker even continued helping BJ for about six more months, finding her a job and an apartment. The case only closed last year."

Daniel looked up at the ceiling, his fingers intertwined as he processed. "So...troubled past, probably early sexual abuse, three children born, domestic violence, and drug use. And yet, she seemed to pull it all together. And now you think she shook her baby?"

"I am not saying that, Daniel.," Jennifer chided. "The evidence seems to point that someone shook this baby, and she is a possibility. I mean, is it possible that this is the unluckiest lady in the world, and her baby just succumbed to a mysterious illness that mimics SBS?" asked Jennifer. "Anything's possible. She suffered so much early trauma; maybe she just continues to get a raw deal out of life. That's where you come in."

"Right. I wonder when the worker saw her last?"

Jennifer flipped through the pages in the chart. "Nine months ago. Everything was fine. That is when she closed the case."

"But if Carrie is six months old, then nine months ago, BJ would have been pregnant. That's not in the record?"

Jennifer flipped through the file again. "Not that I can see."

"Interesting. Was she hiding it from the worker, or did she not even know herself? Well, maybe I can find out the rest of the story when I see her today." Daniel rose. "Okay, I'm heading over to USA."

"Keep me in the loop, Daniel," Jennifer reminded him. "If the baby doesn't make it, you know the state will be all over this case."

"I'll call you this afternoon with an update."

Jennifer waved him out. Feeling confident that his work would be thorough, she shifted her attention to the taller pile and began reviewing cases for closure.

3

The Boy

The kitchen door burst open, jarring him awake. With a deep groan, the boy attempted to sit up. How could it be morning? He had just closed his eyes. His arms hung at his side like great blocks of dead wood, and his face burned like fire. The pain inside of his head pushed out everything else: hunger, cold... even fear. When the room was suddenly illuminated, he squinted in protest.

She's coming.

He didn't pretend to be asleep this time, resting his heavy head against the deep freezer. She carried something as she descended, holding the object in both hands, which blurred out of focus. The glare of the lights hurt his eyes and his brain. Wordlessly, he watched as she started walking toward the furnace—toward him.

"Get up, boy." She called, stopping right in front of him. "Are you going to sleep the whole day away?"

Waves of pain shot through him as he looked up at her. He couldn't remember ever feeling this sick since she put him in the basement. His eyes didn't want to focus on anything, and his body clenched with a deep aching.

"Voila!" she cried, placing the tray on top of the deep freezer and dragging over a folding chair from the corner.

"Boy!" she spoke again. "Get up and get yourself into this chair. Momma made you some breakfast."

Confusion filled his mind with jumbles of words that did not make sense. He tried to speak, but no sound came out.

"What is wrong with you, boy?" she asked. "Shake out those cobwebs and get up for breakfast. It's Halloween!"

He tried to sit up, but a wave of nausea washed over him, and he began to dry heave. She screamed in revulsion.

"Good God, Boy! Are you sick? What is the matter with you?"

His head felt like it would explode, and his throat burned like the time she poured the soap down it.

He tried to speak, but it came out like a croak. "Waaater."

"Boy, if you are sick, you will miss Halloween. Now lookie-here, I brought you some water. Let me get it for you."

She returned with a bottle of water and held it out. He wanted to take it, but his arms remained motionless. With a frustrated click of the tongue, she held the bottle to his cracked lips and poured a little into his open mouth. The cool liquid scorched his raw throat.

He swallowed and formed the words "More."

She poured a little more into his mouth. This time, the burn was less, and he could feel the cool liquid on his tongue and dribbling down his chin.

"Jesus! You must be thirsty. Hey!" she exclaimed when he grabbed the bottle and began drinking greedily. After a few gulps, he choked and began to sputter.

"Slow down," she warned. "You act like you never drank water before." He listened for the anger and the words… but she smiled. "You really ought to drink more water. It's good for you."

"Now I have lots of things to do before tonight, so get up in the chair and eat your breakfast." She turned again to the freezer and returned with the tray. He saw a bowl of oatmeal, a banana, and a spoon.

He shook his head slowly.

But his hunger, which had been ignored for so long, suddenly roared back to life from deep inside his belly.

Then he watched in horror as she turned her back to him and walked away.

She wasn't going to give it to him. It WAS a trick. She was going to take the food back upstairs. He stretched out his small arm toward her and begged, "Please."

"This will do," she announced, picking up a rusted patio table and placing the tray on the top. She moved the table and tray over to where he now sat, saliva forming in his mouth.

"Okay, here it is," she stated. "You get on up and eat your breakfast now." Without waiting for a reply, she continued, "Are you all set?" Her face suddenly lit up, she squealed, and she started clapping her hands.

He simply stared at her.

"Good! I am going to the store to get more candy for the kids! This year, I am dressing up as a witch! You watch how scared they will be when I come out the door to give them the treats!"

She turned on her heels and ascended back to the warmth and light of the kitchen. As her steps receded, he expected the light to recede with her and the darkness to claim him once again. But it didn't. It made no sense, which unsettled the boy. However, before he could try and figure things out, his stomach roared again.

Pulling himself up, he slowly walked to the little table. The pain in his head, now a fierce pounding, did not deter him. His gaze took in the steamy cereal, the melting pat of butter on top. Dizzy with desire, he broke off a small piece of banana, smelled it, and nervously popped it into his mouth. The sweetness of the fruit almost made him cry. Suspicions aside, he put another chunk of banana into his mouth, groaning with pleasure after each bite. He shoved a spoonful of oatmeal into his mouth while it still held banana and marveled at the combination. The warning bells blared in his brain. But he could not hear them because his groans of pleasure and satisfaction drowned out everything else.

4

Daniel

Daniel drove down Springhill Avenue beneath the canopy of moss-laden oaks that lined the divided street. The antebellum homes of mid- and downtown Mobile opened a visual portal to a much older South when cotton ruled the Confederacy. He glanced at the Azalea Trail Maids posing in front of a beautifully restored Greek Revival. He figured it must be time for the annual tourism calendar, wondering how much the teens' extravagant costumes cost their parents.

As he turned off the main road, the University of South Alabama Women and Children's Hospital loomed into view, bringing him out of his revelry and back to the purpose of the drive. A child would very likely die today, and he needed to find out what happened and who was responsible.

Daniel entered the emergency room entrance, nodding at the receptionist, whose brightly colored name tag declared her to be Madelyn. She wore her steel-colored hair in a tight bun at the nape of her neck. The smile served up to Daniel appeared genuine.

"May I help you, sir?"

Daniel produced his badge, which she took and studied closely.

Madelyn peered at the picture through the thick lenses of her large reading glasses, then looked at the man before her. "How can I help you, Mr. Bradshaw?"

Daniel flashed a crooked smile. "I'm here in response to a call from Carol Blessing. Could you please let her know that I am here?"

"Of course. Please take a seat over there," she motioned to a bank of hardback seats in the lobby. "I will call her right now."

He sat as instructed and heard her speak in a muffled tone to the party on the other end of the telephone. When she cradled the receiver, she called out to him. "Mr. Bradshaw? Mrs. Blessing is on her way down to get you."

Daniel wanted to thank her but noticed her attention had turned to the next person in the queue.

Several minutes later, the elevator opened, and Carol Blessing emerged, spying him before heading his way at a clipped pace. As he watched her approach, Daniel realized that Carol always seemed to be in a hurry. At almost six feet tall, Carol had the broad shoulders and narrow waist of an athlete. He wondered if she played sports in college, maybe track and field.

"Daniel," she called out as she reached him. "I'm glad to see you."

"Hi, Carol," he responded and leaned in to ask quietly, "Who is the new receptionist?"

Carol looked around, fixing her gaze upon Madelyn before shrugging. "Who knows? We had some problems with staffing down here. Nobody wants to do intake in the ER. So, hospital administration contracted with the Alabama Area on Aging to provide retired citizens with the opportunity to volunteer. They rotate in and out. I can't keep up with them."

"I can see it's a win-win for the hospital. You know, free labor and all."

Carol agreed. "It is good for the budget. But it is also good for them. By giving a little of their time, they're able to stave off the stagnation that often plagues the elderly."

"Good idea," Daniel conceded. "Keep me in mind when I retire around age 80."

"I'll make a note," she quipped. "But I hope to God I am already on a tropical beach by then.

"I am not really here to question your hiring practices, my friend. I am here about the Ossie case."

Carol managed a sad smile. "When I said it was good to see you, I meant it. I am so glad that they sent you. This baby will not make it. I'm not saying the doctor has called it. It's just that I have seen this injury all too often."

"Shaken Baby?"

She nodded. "As I said, the doctor is really not ready to call SBS yet. But, from my experience, that is definitely what it looks like. And that poor mother cannot stop crying. You know I do feel sorry for the lady; it's obvious she's in a lot of pain. But I have to wonder if the emotions are as much guilt as sadness."

"That's what I hope we can find out."

"I will take you to the unit," she said as she led him into the elevator.

"I read the report," began Daniel as they rode up. "But fill me in on all that has happened here… beginning with when the child entered the hospital."

Carol nodded, familiar with the process of reporting out.

"At 3:45 am, Carrie Ossie, a six-month-old Caucasian infant, arrived by ambulance, accompanied by her mother, Betty Jo Ossie. The child was unresponsive, and her lips were cyanotic. The child had no marks, bruises, or lacerations on her body. She appeared to be well-kempt and on target with height and weight. When her breathing became labored, she was intubated and is now in PICU in critical condition."

"What about the petechial hemorrhages?" he asked.

"Yes, there were petechial hemorrhages, but as I just mentioned, we are not yet ready to signify Shaken Baby Syndrome. Doctor Lambert is with the baby now. She wants to do a CT, not just of the head, but a whole skeletal workup as well to see if there are old broken bones."

Daniel, aware that it was common practice to look for old injuries in cases like this, asked. "So, where is mom now?"

Carol pointed to the waiting room outside of the PICU area. "She is in there while the doctor is with Carrie. Mom had been crying for hours. The last time I peeked, she was just staring at the floor with a blank affect."

Dan pursed his lips. "Is there an empty room where she and I could talk privately?

Carol paused momentarily, "I know you sometimes use a dictation room. We have a couple on each floor, so the doctors don't have to return to their office between visits."

Daniel smiled. "If one is free, that would be great. Point me to it."

Carol took him to a small office, sparsely furnished with a desk and two chairs. After opening the door for him, Carol turned and walked briskly back down the hall.

Daniel dropped his satchel on the floor beneath his chair. After placing a legal notepad and two pens on the desk, he left the office to find BJ Ossie, hoping she would shed some light on why her baby girl lay dying in a hospital crib.

5

Jennifer

Jennifer frowned at the light tapping on her office door. She had been reviewing a completed investigation for closure. She immersed herself in the narrative to process the case flow, making mental notes of discrepancies that required more follow-up. So, unnecessary disruptions annoyed her.

"Come in," she called without turning her head from the screen.

"Hey, Jennifer," Kim began. But stopped when she saw her supervisor facing the computer screen.

Aware of the silence, Jennifer regarded the worker standing patiently in the doorway. "Yes? What is it, Kim? How did it go at Providence?"

"I see you are reading an investigation summary, so I can hang tight 'til you are through."

"Well, it's one of your CA/Ns, and I just finished it."

With the press of a button, the report disappeared from the screen, relegated to somewhere in the digital world of DHR.

"Jennifer turned away from the computer. "See? I'm all yours. What about the broken arm?"

"Oh," Kim waved her hand in a dismissive gesture. "Turns out the X-rays proved that the little tyke has a condition called brittle bone disease. They are keeping him overnight to educate the parents on protective measures. I could give you all the details, but the bottom line is– not abuse."

Jennifer said, "Hmmm. I have seen kids with brittle bones; poor kid will have to be careful his entire life. Thanks for checking it out,

Kim. I am glad we have a good outcome." She started to turn back to her computer and noticed the worker still in the doorway.

"Was there anything else?"

Kim shifted her feet before answering. "Yes, um, while I was at Providence, I ran into Detective Green."

"How is he?" Jennifer asked. "I haven't seen him since he went to the Domestic Violence Task Force."

Kim cleared her throat. "He seemed right as rain. He wanted me to tell you howdy and to let you know about something. Do you remember Candy Monroe?"

Jennifer looked at her quizzically. "Of course I do. I worked with her a few years ago. She is in nursing school in South Alabama now. Why?"

The worker looked down at the floor.

"What is it, Kim?"

"Detective Green told me that Candy Monroe was killed two days ago by her boyfriend."

Jennifer had been leaning in her chair but suddenly bolted upright and pounded both palms on the desk. "What? How?"

Kim nodded, "He said you would want to know."

"Was he sure it was her?" Jennifer asked, already knowing the answer. Detective Green had also worked closely with Candy and would not have misidentified her. Slowly, she sank back into the chair and asked again, "What happened?"

"I don't rightly know all the details. I ran into Detective Green as I was heading into Providence. He told me about Candy. You know...that she used to be a foster child and asked me to tell you. But I was in a hurry and didn't get the details."

When she received no comment, she rushed on. "I didn't know you had been her worker. I just thought you were familiar with her case on account of you being a supervisor. I should have asked more questions. I am so sorry."

Jennifer straightened up. "No. There's nothing for you to be sorry for. Green was right; I did want to know."

"Detective Green said if you wanted details, you could give him a call."

Jennifer didn't answer. Staring at her desk blotter, she muttered, "I just can't believe it. She was one of the lucky ones who made it out of the system."

Suddenly aware that she was talking to herself, Jennifer looked up sheepishly and shot her investigator a crooked smile. "Thanks for telling me. I will call Detective Green and get the details. Again, glad your emergency turned out to be a false alarm."

Jennifer turned back to her screen, and Kim knew it was her cue to leave.

As she stared at the blank computer screen in front of her, Jennifer tried to process the information she had just been given. It just made no sense. Candy was a success story. This shouldn't have happened. Candy was dead.

The jingle of the phone jolted her to the present.

"Jennifer Riley."

"Hey, Jen. It's Mason." His voice, rough from years of smoking Marlboro Reds, brought back a flood of warm feelings.

Mason Green was a detective with the Mobile Police Department. When she was a sexual abuse investigator, they worked many cases together and formed a bond of mutual respect. She had always admired his ability to relate and investigate such complex cases as the incest ones they inevitably shared.

"Hey, Mason, I was just about to call you."

"Yeah. Kim just hit me up and told me you were pretty upset about Candy. I knew you would be. When I went into that house and saw Candy, I got so mad, I wanted to kill that SOB myself, save the taxpayers some money."

"Mason, what happened? She was doing so well!"

"According to her friends, Candy aced her classes and became popular with the other nursing students. Her study group even voted her to be the team leader."

"But that's exactly what I am talking about, Mason," Jennifer interrupted. "She survived her abusive stepfather, navigated through the broken child welfare system, and actually made it! How did this happen?"

Mason was silent for a moment.

"I'm sorry, please go on. I think I am just in shock,"

"No, I get it," his voice softened. "A senseless act like this shouldn't happen. But apparently, Candy's boyfriend wasn't too thrilled with her popularity. Some boy in the study group would text Candy often about tutoring him for the anatomy class. The boyfriend found the texts, became paranoid, and demanded she quit the group."

"Did she?"

"No. In his statement, he confessed that she threatened to break up with him if he couldn't get his jealousy under control. An argument broke out, and he clobbered her over the head with his practice bat."

"Practice bat?"

"Yeah, get this. Son of a Bitch was on the church softball team. How's that for irony?"

Jennifer couldn't speak. Her mind was flooded with images of young Candy Monroe and all she had overcome.

"Jen? You still there?" Green asked.

"Yes, I'm here," she whispered. "I still just can't believe it."

"Hell, I'm sorry Jen. I know how much you did for her; how proud you were. I knew it would hit you hard."

"She did it for herself," Jennifer corrected. "She got her life on track and went to school to make something of herself."

"Yeah. And all it took was one piece of scum to end it all."

Jennifer didn't answer, as a lump formed in her throat.

Green continued. "Hey, I found out there will be a service at South-side Funeral Home this afternoon late if you are interested. I think it's at four."

"I wouldn't know what to say," Jennifer stammered.

"Well, just wanted to pass it on to you. No one would blame you if you didn't go. Her crazy family will be there probably, and I wouldn't be sad if I never saw them again."

"I will think about it." She cleared her throat. "Thank you, Mason, for letting me know."

"Sarge is calling me. Gotta fly. Take care, and let's have lunch soon, okay?"

Jennifer replied, "Sure, Mason, that would be nice."

Then, the line disconnected.

Jennifer stared at the telephone receiver as if it were a foreign object. Flashing images of Candy's face flooded her mind unbidden. She remembered how happy Candy had been at her high school commencement. And how proud Jennifer felt to see her foster child, decked out in a black graduation gown, holding up her diploma folder like a trophy!

"Look at this, Ms. Riley!" Candy had exclaimed, "Guess you never thought you'd see this day!"

Jennifer protested. "I knew you had it in you, Candy. Your ability to achieve everything you want is only limited by your own fears."

Candy pretended to roll her eyes… "How many times have I heard that one? Maybe you should cross-stitch it on a pillow and give it to me."

Jennifer smiled at the young woman. "I would if I could cross-stitch and if I thought it would sink in."

Then they both laughed as Candy's foster mother started taking pictures.

The harsh sound of the 'busy' signal alerted Jennifer that she had not hung up the phone. She quickly replaced the receiver to silence the noise.

"Come on Jen, get a grip," she said out loud. "You have got to snap out of this."

It was unprofessional to get so emotional. Today was the end of the month, and there was so much more to accomplish that day to get the cases approved. Mentally steeling herself, she reached for another case and began reading it for closure. But the images of Candy continued to invade her thoughts. Concentration would be useless unless she addressed this feeling. Once she had made the decision, her mind immediately felt less chaotic. A sense of calm validated her path.

Jennifer emailed her staff that she would be out of the office for a few hours but assured them that she would return in the evening to close their cases. Grabbing her purse, she strode purposefully out of the building.

6

Daniel

Daniel stood in the doorway of the PICU waiting room, studying the woman slumped over in her chair. She stared at the floor as if trying to find meaning within the gray-speckled tiles. From his record review, Daniel knew that she was 24 years old, but BJ Ossie looked at least 10 years older. Her blonde hair hung lifeless and limp on her shoulders. She was extremely thin and wore a loose-fitting sundress and house shoes, her bare arms covered in scabbed-over sores.

"Ms. Ossie?" he began.

She looked up at him blankly, her eyes flat.

"Yes?" she responded tenuously.

"I'm Daniel Bradshaw with Mobile County DHR." He showed her his badge and watched as understanding and then wariness crept into her eyes. He continued. "I would like to talk with you about Carrie."

"Is she dead?"

Caught off guard by her question, he answered quickly. "No, ma'am. She is still with the Doctor. I just need to ask you a few questions. Let's go down the hall where we can talk privately."

She got up slowly without a word and began to follow him, her house slippers echoing a whoosh and a slap for each step.

Daniel led her to the interview room and pulled out the chair for her. She settled in, rubbing her hands together to disguise the tremors. Her eyes widened when she saw him pick up the notepad and pen. Daniel kept his voice calm and steady to put her more at ease.

"Ms. Ossie," he began. "I hear you liked to be called BJ. Would you prefer me to call you that?"

She shook her head, "Yes, sir. I mean, it's whatever you want."

"BJ, I need to ask you a few questions about how Carrie came to be here. It is important for me to hear your information and to get it right. I will take some notes to ensure I don't miss a thing. Okay?"

When she nodded her assent, he continued.

"Tell me everything that happened before Carrie came to the hospital."

She looked nervous again. "Like before when?"

"Just start with your day yesterday. Did you get the other kids to school in the morning?"

"Well," she began slowly, her eyes casting back to the floor. You know, I only just got the two now. Bennie got adopted when he was a baby."

"Okay, I will make a note of that. So yesterday…"

She coughed nervously. "I wasn't feeling so good yesterday. I had a bug or sumpin.' So, I got up late, maybe nine or so."

"What time do you usually wake up?"

She made a snorting sound that could have been a laugh. "Ever since my Carrie came along, I get up with the chickens. That young'un doesn't let me get any rest. She's up and hollering 'bout six or so."

"But yesterday was different?" prodded Daniel.

"Yeah. Like I said, I got up around nine. There was a god-awful mess in the kitchen when I walked in, too."

"A mess?"

She raised her head, a glint of amusement as she shared the memory. "My boy, Jason had gone and done got into the Fruit Loops whilst I was still sleeping. That whole dad-blamed box was poured out on the floor. And that idiot child was just sitting on the floor, eating them with his hands." Her lips twisted into a strained smile. "It was a sight, I tell you."

Daniel smiled at her. "Sounds like it. What did you do?"

"I whacked his ass and told him to get to the table with his food."

When Daniel was silent, she added quickly, "I mean, I didn't hit him hard or anything. Just a little love tap, you know."

She watched Daniel to see if he would react. But his questions continued in the same calm manner. "Carrie hadn't woken up yet?"

BJ shook her head. "Oh, No. Mr. Daniel, I plum forgot to tell you Carrie wasn't home the night before. That's why I got to get myself some better sleep. The girl had spent the night at her daddy's house."

"Brian MacArthur?" Daniel asked, looking down at his notes.

She snorted again. "Naw. Brian's Jason's dad. Gil is Carrie's daddy."

Daniel wrote 'Gil' on the pad with a question mark and asked, "What is Gil's last name? Are you two together now?"

"Gil Carrollton. And no, we ain't together. Never really WERE together if you know what I mean; on account he is married. But I went to the Child Support office when the baby was born to get him to help me out. Now I got child support, but the judge said he gets to see her."

Daniel nodded. "I will need his address and phone number as well. He will need to answer some questions since Carrie was with him."

Flipping the pad for a fresh page, he asked. "What time did Gil bring Carrie home?"

She shrugged. "I dunno. He dropped her off on his way to work 'bout 10:30. He was working an 11-3 shift that day and running late, so he just handed her to me like a football and took off."

"And how did she seem when he returned her?"

"Fine, I reckon. Yeah, just fine."

"Was there something that bothered you or seemed out of the ordinary?" he queried.

Still looking down, she shook her head. "He doesn't really care nothing bout Carrie. I think he takes his visits just for spite."

"What makes you think that?"

She didn't answer, and her gaze dropped again.

Daniel decided to press on. "BJ, let's move on for right now."

Summarizing, he said, "Gil brought Carrie home around 10:30 on his way to work, and she seemed fine. What happened after that? Where was Jason?"

"Oh, I forgot to say that too. I swear, my mind is just so foggy. I can't get my story straight. Jason was at the mommy's day out."

"What is Mommy's Day Out?"

"It's like free babysitting at Christ United Methodist for mommies who need a few hours break during the day. I took him there before Carrie got home cuz, like I done said, I was sick."

Daniel paused, hoping she would fill in the gap. Years ago, he had learned that people were uncomfortable with silence. Sometimes, the best way to let an interview progress is to remain quiet.

BJ quickly complied. "Yeah, so when Carrie got home, I made her a cereal bottle and put her in the Johnny jumper so I could lay back down."

Daniel felt like he was pulling teeth, trying to get a steady stream of information for the timeline. But he continued gently, afraid she would get scared and shut down. "Then?"

"Um, I heard her fussin' bout 12 or so, so I got on up. I had to go get Jason anyway, so I got my neighbor, Mrs. Katz, to keep an eye on Carrie."

"I will need her full name and phone number as well," Daniel explained. "It is important for us to establish a timeline and talk to everyone who was with Carrie yesterday."

"Ida May Katz is the widder woman who lives next door to us—a real nice black lady who watches Carrie sometimes."

Daniel jotted down the information. "You picked up Jason from daycare and brought him home?" summarized Daniel.

She looked up again but did not meet his eyes. Her body stiffened. "Well, not straight home. You see, I was startin' to feel a little better, and I was bored just sittin' around the house, so Jason and I went to hang out with friends of mine. We didn't get back 'til almost eight at night."

His eyes narrowed, but he continued in the same even tone. "I will need these friends' names and contact information too."

BJ's head jerked up, her ennui changing into something else. Her voice remained flat but with a tinge of anxiety as her speech quickened. "Oh, wait," she said. "You know what, Mr. Daniel? I don't know what the Sam-hell I am talking about. That was Saturday when Jason and I went to see my friends, not yesterday. I'm just all mixed up in the head."

"So, you weren't visiting friends?" he repeated the obvious lie.

"No, not this afternoon. Jason and me went to that park, the one with the ducks you can feed."

"Municipal Park?" Daniel offered?

"Yep, that's the one. Yeah. We hung out for a long time, just feeding those ducks. I don't know why I said the other thing. I'm all out of sorts right now on account of Carrie being sick."

Daniel decided to get her entire statement before confronting the contradictions.

"So, you and Jason got home from the park around 8 pm," he repeated.

"Yeah. Bout then." BJ's voice lost its edge and became less pressured. "Picked up Carrie from Miss Katz's house and took the kids home. I was so tuckered out; we all just went to bed."

"When did you notice Carrie was ill?" Daniel pressed on.

BJ turned away for a moment. When she looked back, Daniel saw tears brimming over her eyes. "Lemme see. I got up to pee around two or so and peeked in on her. That's when I knew something was wrong. I mean, she was so still and looked blue!"

Daniel placed his notepad down and looked at her kindly. "That must have been terrifying for you."

Flowing freely, the tears were accompanied by small hiccupping sobs. "Oh, Mr. Daniel, I was so scared! I… I… ran over to Miss Katz's house… to… to call the ambulance on account of I ain't got… got no phone. I rode with my ba-baby in the ambulance all the way here."

She let out a plaintive wail, which disintegrated into convulsive sobs.

Daniel waited while she cried, handing her the small box of Kleenex he kept in his briefcase and placing a conciliatory hand on her shoulder. Paying close attention as she switched back and forth between flat monotone and agitation, he suspected she was using meth or some type of drug and knew he would have to test her. But something else bothered him about her story. When her sobs subsided, he asked her.

"BJ, where is Jason now?"

She looked up quickly, eyes still wet but the wariness returning. "Um, His daddy came over and stayed with him while I came to the hospital."

"Brian McArthur? Don't you have a PFA against him?"

She wiped her eyes with a tissue and fixed an uncomfortable smile. "Oh, he got himself some help. He doesn't do those bad things anymore. A boy needs his dad, you know, so I let him back into Jason's life."

Daniel chewed his bottom lip and steered the conversation toward the drugs.

"BJ, "he began after several minutes.

She had resumed staring at the floor, but when she looked up, he noticed that her shaking was becoming more pronounced.

"How long have you been back on crystal meth?" he asked pointedly.

Fear colored her cheeks red as the rest of her face paled. Her voice quivered. "What do you mean? I don't use drugs! I stopped years ago!"

"Yes, I read your file," he stated. "I know that you had a substance abuse problem earlier in life and saw that you had treatment and became sober. That took a lot of courage and strength."

He paused. "But, BJ, I see the meth sores on your arms, and your whole body is shaking. I need to drug test you today to ensure that you are not under the influence of drugs while caring for your children."

Her voice became shrill–panicked. "You can't make me drug test! You can't make me do anything! I know my damn rights!"

Continuing in a low, calm voice, Daniel said. "No. I cannot force you to take the drug test. Only a judge can do that. However, at this time, I can't allow you to have contact with your children until I am sure that you are not under the influence of drugs. Now, I can file a motion in court to have you drug tested, and we will do a hair follicle test that will go back three months."

He stopped again to let his words sink in before continuing: "BJ, I am not trying to scare you or bully you; I am just stating the facts. From the limited time we've talked, I can see that you love your children."

She nodded rapidly, tears and mucus smeared on her face.

"I want us to work together to see how we can keep your children safe and help your family be together. But I will need to know what's really going on so that I can help you, Jason, and Carrie."

She began to cry again. Racking sobs caused her whole body to shake.

Daniel allowed her to process all that he had said.

After several minutes, she looked up again, her eyes red and puffy but her face resolute.

"You're right. I did start back with the meth again about two months ago," she began.

When Daniel just nodded his head, she continued.

"After I got pregnant, no one had a whit of time for me. Gill dumped me. My friends thought I was a skank for getting knocked-up by a married man. I just wanted to feel better. I got so desperate; I called Brian. And you know what, Mr. Daniel? He told me that he had never forgotten me. He said he wanted to see me and Jason again."

"You were lonely, and he was Jason's dad."

"And one thing turned into another… you know what I mean?"

Daniel let silence fill the gap until she continued.

"But he lied." She shook her head. "He hadn't changed. He was still using drugs, still mean as a snake. And not just meth, he was shooting H too."

"When did you find out?" probed Daniel.

"One night, he took me to hang with his friends, and they were smoking meth. He passed the pipe to me, and I didn't want to piss him off. So, I did it. And that's all it took. I started using again."

Daniel asked softly. "Did Brian move back in?"

She shook her head. "No, he has his own place."

"And that is where you and Jason went yesterday," stated Daniel.

Her eyes welled up again. "Yes, we went there, and I smoked meth. Brian wanted to see his son and I was jonesing for a fix."

Daniel said even more softly. "Did Brian come home with you last night?"

She nodded wordlessly.

Finally, Daniel asked the question. "Did Brian hurt Carrie?"

She jumped up. "No! No, Mr. Daniel, No! Neither one of us hurt my baby! I tell you, she wouldn't wake up! I got to go! I got to go to the bathroom right now!"

She pulled at the door and rushed down the hall before he could say anything else.

He knew she would not be back for some time, if at all. Daniel made more notes on his pad, then went in search of Carrie's doctor.

He found Dr. Lambert standing in the hall, writing in a chart. A male nurse waited patiently and silently next to her, apparently needing the medication change or diagnostic test order that was being hastily scrawled. Daniel eyed the older doctor appreciatively.

Dr. Vivian Lambert, a pediatrician with a specialty in child abuse cases, diagnosed children who were in the hospital on suspicion of non-accidental injuries. Daniel had worked with her as she had uncovered some severe incidents of child abuse that had been dismissed by local law enforcement as accidental. However, she had also proven accidental cases when parents were charged with abuse.

Handing the completed chart over to the nurse, Dr. Lambert looked up at Daniel and smiled.

"Daniel," she acknowledged.

"Hi, Dr. Lambert. I am here about Carrie Ossie. I wondered if the skeletal survey had come back?"

The smile left her face. "Not yet, I am afraid. But so far, the signs point to SBS. There was no other trauma to her body, so I'm not ruling it conclusive until I get the scans."

Daniel nodded and continued. "But you observed retinal hemorrhaging. Isn't that a sign of Shaken Baby Syndrome?"

"Yes. I noted pretty significant bleeding and have no doubt that this baby suffered a brain injury." Her face hardened. "With all the education out there about how dangerous it is to shake a baby; I just don't get why parents continue to think it is acceptable discipline."

"These are some of the hardest cases," Daniel agreed. "What is Carrie's prognosis? Will she pull through?"

Dr. Lambert shook her head. "I will be surprised if she makes it through the night."

She added quickly. "The body is an amazing thing, though, and I could be wrong. But I don't think that will happen this time. The damage to her brain is just too severe."

Daniel asked. "Did you do a tox screen?"

"Yes, it might take a week or two to come back."

"One more question, and I will leave you alone," Daniel smiled.

"Nonsense, anything I can give you to help, please feel free to ask."

"Did anyone other than the mother come in with the baby?"

Dr. Lambert frowned again. "No. I understand from the nurse, that the mother tried to call the baby's father, but he has not shown up. I guess he was not just that interested." She gave a grunt of disgust.

"Hmmm. That is strange. Okay, I will try to find Ms. Ossie again and finish our talk. Please let me know if you get any more information or if the child takes a turn for the worse."

"Will do, Daniel." Dr. Lambert smiled and picked up another chart out of the rack.

Daniel pulled out his cell phone, ignoring the "NO CELL PHONES " sign on the wall. The nurse glared at him, but she just shrugged when he showed her his badge. The phone rang several times before he heard the voice.

"Daniel, I was hoping you would check in. What did you find out?"

"Hi, Jennifer, it's not good. I will fill you in when I get back. But for now, can you get Kim or Michael to go to the Ossie house? The boyfriend, Brian, is supposed to be there with Jason, and according to Ms. Ossie, he is coming down off meth or heroin. Apparently, he has been using both. She will need to take the police with her because I'm afraid they will need to do a pick-up."

Jennifer jotted down the notes as he spoke: "Okay. I got it. I will call it in and have them pick up the little boy. Kim is free right now, so I will fill her in and send her off. When will you be able to talk?"

"I am trying to finish up my interview with Ms. Ossie, who just admitted to using drugs as well. By tomorrow, we will most likely be looking at a child's death."

"Oh, No. That poor child!" Jennifer said. "You finish up with her, and I will make sure Jason is safe."

"Thanks, Sup. That little boy is going to be so upset. Make sure Kim is prepared for that."

"Can you imagine what his young life has been like?" she answered.

Jennifer returned to the subject at hand. "Listen, I will send Kim first to family court with a petition for a pickup order for both children in case the baby makes it. Tell the hospital that no one is allowed to see the baby without supervision until we can unravel all of this.

When she gets the pickup order, Kim will call the police to accompany her to take custody of Jason."

Daniel agreed. "It is tragic that in the wake of this horrible situation, this mother will likely lose both of her children."

"The ripple effect of abuse on families is always devastating," Jennifer agreed.

"Jennifer, I have to go. I see Ms. Ossie coming down the hall and need to return to my interview. I will catch you up when I return to the office this afternoon."

"It may be closer to six when we can meet. I am on the way to a funeral right now."

Daniel's voice softened. "Oh, Jennifer, I am sorry. Was it a close friend?"

Jennifer felt her throat constrict. "It was a former foster child."

She heard his intake of breath. "Wow, again, so sorry to hear that. I have been there, and it really sucks to see someone that you have really tried to help give up and lose the fight."

Jennifer sat quietly for a minute, angry at herself for the tears that formed in her eyes. Daniel had hit the nail on the head, but she wasn't ready for the emotion. She steeled herself. "Yes, it is very hard. But I will be back by 6, so if you are in, we can chat."

Daniel snorted. "Oh, I will definitely be working late tonight. See you then."

And the line was disconnected.

7

Jennifer

Jennifer chose an aisle seat in the back row of the small salon. Scanning the room, she felt disappointed that so few people had come to say goodbye. She recognized Candy's foster parent, Greta Handy, and watched as a flash of relief transformed the older woman's somber face when she spied Jennifer as well.

For 15 years, Greta had fostered teenagers, providing them with the love and nurturing most of them never got from their own families. She looked like a postcard grandmother and believed that the way to help abused children was to love them unconditionally. Unfortunately, parenting troubled teens could often become incredibly stressful. The frustration of trying to get through to those who had built up years of solid walls often took its toll. When they had reached their wit's end, some other foster parents gave up on the hardest teens with the most defiant behaviors. Not Greta. She would dig in her heels, grit her teeth, and just keep trying, demonstrating a rare understanding that the anger they spewed came from previous trauma and fear of rejection.

Candy tried her best to derail Greta's belief in her. During her years with Ms. Greta, the angry teen displayed defiance, rebellion, and mistrust. Yet Greta never wavered in her message. She told Candy every day that she was smart, she was good, she was safe, and she was loved. Little by little, Jennifer watched as Candy's 'fight-flight-freeze' response settled down, as she began to trust that Greta meant her words. Had it not been for Greta, Candy would have disappeared into the broken child welfare system, moving from home to home and believing more with each subsequent move that she had no worth. Jennifer enjoyed working with Greta. Together, they had finally gotten through to Candy. Or so Jennifer had thought.

Greta plopped down next to the Social Worker on the weathered pew. Jennifer nodded to her with a smile, offering a side hug to the buxom lady. Out of the corner of her eye, she saw movement. The faces of those who framed Candy's early life drew her gaze. Standing beside the podium, talking with each other in hushed tones, were Candy's family: her mother, stepfather, and two older brothers. Their faces, concrete masks, seemed to hold the same terrible secret Jennifer had seen in Candy's eyes when they met. More than once, Candy's mother looked at her with surprise. Jennifer just met the other woman's eyes evenly, feeling the slow anger building. She probably didn't think I would come, Jennifer thought. When Deena's husband noted the staring contest, he jerked his wife away around with a practiced hand.

"Good afternoon. I am Cyrus Johnson, and I will be officiating the service." The voice was deep bass, slow, methodical, and, yes, practiced. Jennifer turned to see the funeral director standing next to her with large brown eyes fringed by thick, long eyelashes. His smile was fixed and practiced, never moving, as if drawn onto his face by a soft crayon. He noticed her silence and continued, "How did you know Miss Munroe?"

"Oh, er," Jennifer tried to think quickly. She could not reveal that Candy was a client due to confidentiality.

"I was a friend, "she lied. Of course, none of Candy's actual friends were in attendance, Jennifer noted sadly. In fact, she counted exactly ten people in the room to mourn the young girl's passing.

"Hmmm." He seemed to consider Jennifer's words. "That's nice. Would you like to say a few words?"

"God, no!" she blurted, then realized it came out too forcefully. "Er, I mean, I am just terrible at public speaking. Besides, I don't know her family (she lied). I just came to pay my respects."

At first, Mr. Johnson looked offended, but he quickly readjusted his face to simulate reflection. "Very well; I am sure the family will appreciate you being here." He then moved on to meet an elderly woman with the pinched face of someone in pain.

The service was simple. Mr. Johnson dispassionately recited basic facts about Candy that he had obviously read off the 5x7 card in his hand. It became noticeably clear that he knew nothing about her. No one spoke about Candy's sense of humor, her ability to see the best in people, and her fierce loyalty to those she cared about. Dammit! She was a real person who was alive and then was not.

When the director asked if anyone else had something to share, no one moved, not even her family. Jennifer wondered sadly why she had even come. But she knew why. She came for Candy. She wanted to get up and say something to these people about the young woman who was so much more than vague platitudes.

But she couldn't speak up. After all, what would she say without giving away their client relationship? Knowing she would remain silent, she practiced what she wanted to say in her head.

"Yes, I knew Candy, ever since she was 12 years old. I am the one who investigated and substantiated her stepfather's sexual abuse of her, then took her away from a mother who didn't even seem to notice. I am the one who raced to the foster home every time she had a meltdown or tried to hurt herself. I thought I had finally gotten through to her and encouraged her to finish high school.

"She even went to college. Candy became strong, resilient, and independent. I am the one who believed she had gotten over all of you. But I was wrong. It didn't matter that she got out. She never escaped your world!"

Jennifer wondered how the smug little family would feel if she did say those things. Would they feel sad for the life that their abuse had destroyed? No. It was better for her to sit quietly and try to find some closure.

The congregation began filing past the open coffin to offer condolences to the family. Jennifer knew she would not be welcomed, so she gathered her purse, hugged Greta tightly, and left the building. Outside, the sun shone brightly, although it had begun the slow dip into the horizon. She heard the song of birds from the oak tree and felt strangely angry that the day had turned out to be beautiful.

Jennifer felt the lump in her throat grow. Why hadn't Candy called her for help? Had she been afraid? Ashamed? Maybe she became resigned to her fate when she realized she had found her stepfather all over again, in a man named David. It was all such a waste.

Her head and neck were aching, which alerted Jennifer that she had been clenching her teeth. She was tired and hungry and remembered skipping lunch to finish up a review. She decided to swing by her apartment for a quick bite before returning to the office and to the task of approving investigations.

By the time she pulled up to her apartment, the sun had sunk even lower in the sky, casting shadows in the grass. Tiny goblins, witches, and superheroes padded from door to door, singing out for candy.

"Oh, crap!" she uttered. She had forgotten that it was Halloween despite the note on her frig reminding her to buy candy. The sprint to her door was short, and she quickly turned off the porch light to signal that she was not handing out treats. "Sorry, kids," she muttered. "Apparently, this year, I am the Grinch who stole Halloween."

Jennifer listened to the low hum of the air conditioner as she entered the dimly lit den. She left off the lights and dropped wearily into a wingback chair. With her eyes closed, Jennifer wrapped the darkness and the easy familiarity of the space around her shoulders like a comfortable old sweater, sighing as the tension began to leave her body. She set her watch for 20 minutes, closed her eyes, and drifted to an exhausted sleep.

8

The Boy

"Rocket," whispered the boy as he stirred awake, the last remnant of a dream playing out on his lips. He had been riding bikes with Billy. They were following the Ice Cream Man whose metallic rendition of Twinkle-Twinkle announced for miles that, for $1.75, you could be eating a bubblegum rocket or an orange push-up. Licking his lips, he could still taste the sugary goodness. As eyelids flickered open, confusion creased his face momentarily before understanding jolted him back. He still sat in the folding chair.

His head, heavy and full of fuzz, still hurt. Bad. His eyes were so heavy that he started to drift off again. Suddenly, his stomach lurched, tightened, and knotted.

"Ow!" he cried out in pain, clutching the midsection of his torso. He tried to get out of the chair and run to the slop bucket, but his legs refused to move. It was like a brick was sitting on his chest and stomach.

And it hurt so bad!

He tried to cry out again, but the darkness slowly crept over him like a blanket.

"Mommy," he whimpered before he lost consciousness again.

When he opened his eyes, the pain was gone. Blinking twice, the blurriness resolved, and his surroundings came into focus.

He was in the kitchen. Billy was there. Daddy was there. Even Momma was there. They were happy. All of them. In the same house. Like before.

Daddy had just come home from the car lot and looked right at Billy.

"Hey, Billy Bob!" he called out. I heard a funny joke at the dealership today. Wanna hear it?"

"Sure, Dad, let's hear it." Billy winked at his little brother.

"Guess what the Easter Bunny drives?" daddy asked.

"I don't know." Billy played along. What does the Easter Bunny drive?"

"A Volkswagens Rabbit."

Billy laughed so hard! He always got daddy's jokes.

The boy spoke up, "Does the Easter Bunny really drive a car?"

Momma called out from the kitchen, her voice light and musical. "Ken dear, dinner is almost ready."

Daddy smiled at the boy and said, "Your mom's fried chicken and rice are the best things in the state! You and Billy go wash up now."

The brothers ran upstairs, and the boy heard his dad say, "Martha, guess what the Easter Bunny drives?"

He blinked again and found himself in Momma's bedroom now. Curtains were drawn tight to keep out the light; the room was dark and chilly. She lay perfectly still, heavy covers pulled over her head. He couldn't even see her breathing. It must be a 'blue' day, as Daddy called them. But he knew sometimes the blue days lasted longer than a day.

He stood beside the bed, gently pulling down the covers to reveal a pale, slack face. When her eyes fluttered open, she touched his arm and said softly, "Go tell your daddy he needs to take care of dinner. Momma's not feeling well."

The boy descended the stairs to pass along her message but stopped short in surprise. Momma somehow beat him downstairs. Laughing and dancing in the living room with Daddy, she motioned for him to join. Billy was clapping along.

Daddy leaned over and kissed her lips. "That's my best girl!" he said.

"Gros, Dad!" protested Billy.

And momma just laughed and danced while the boy looked on.

Suddenly, they were all at the ball field watching Billy's little league game. Up at bat, Billy winked at him before hitting a line drive down centerfield and rounding the bases fast as a bullet. That was Billy... the superstar.

He watched his big brother, so proud of him, when he heard a voice.

"Why don't you play baseball?" said a girl in the stands. "Are you slow?"

He shook his head. "Momma says I just ain't big enough yet."

"I think there is something wrong with you," she persisted.

"There's nothing wrong with me," he yelled back at her.

Then the clouds darkened, and lightning shot out. Fear gripped the boy as he watched the storm approach. He knew what happened next, but there was nothing he could do but watch death come for Billy.

Groaning, he slowly woke again. Nausea gripped him, and he heaved onto the cement floor. Spewing out bits of banana and oatmeal, the boy continued to vomit until weakened; he slumped onto the floor.

The cement felt cool on his forehead, for which he was grateful. Willing the pain to go away, he failed to notice the transition from dusk to dark. His tiny body started shaking from his head to his gut. Clutching his stomach, he groaned again.

Then a sound filled his ears: children laughing, screaming in delight, and calling out, "Trick or Treat!" He listened as if from far away; his momma erupted in high-pitched laughter and cries of delight. She marveled over each little monster or angel that came to her door. A wet sensation on his cheeks surprised him. He hadn't really cried in so long that he had forgotten what it felt like as the salty drops rolled down his face and landed on his lips.

The pain intensified. I must be dying, he thought, without fear. Is this how Billy felt when he died? He seemed detached, like watching himself from the ceiling as the throbbing ache rose higher and higher: up from his tummy, into his chest, and finally his throat before it exploded.

9

The Boy

Brenda Pace, six years old and dressed as Princess Jasmine, ran ahead of her mother toward the house.

"Bren," called her mother. "You wait for me right now, young lady, or we will go back to our house for good."

Brenda paused and looked impatiently at her mother, sighing audibly. "Mom, you know the Barry house is cool! She has that scary skeleton and gives the best candy on the block. Her porch light is on, so HURRY UP!"

Tiffany Place looked annoyed as she walked deliberately slower to teach her daughter some manners. How did kids today learn to talk like that to their parents? She had to admit that she was mildly surprised to see the Barry light on. She had wondered if Martha would engage in Halloween this year.

"Tiffany! Wait up!" Beth Youngman ran up to her friend, a dark-haired little boy in tow. "Ricky, go up there and say hey to Brenda while the grown-ups talk."

As he ran ahead of them, catching up to Brenda, the two friends settled into a slower pace. Tiffany pointed to the Barry house.

"I can't believe Martha is doing Halloween as usual," she said.

"Right? Martha always said Halloween was her favorite holiday, but after all that had happened, I can't believe she is giving out candy."

Tiffany agreed. "First, Billy's death. Then, that jerk of a husband took the younger boy and moved out. What that poor woman has endured."

Beth whispered, "To hear it from Harriet Ponder, who lives next door, Martha has completely lost it. Harriet said that sometimes she can hear Martha talking, even yelling at herself in the house."

"Harriet Ponder is an evil gossip. I just wish she would put herself into Martha's shoes."

Beth laughed. "You're probably right. She's the one who spread the lies about Pastor West."

"Hmmm. I hope they were lies," Tiffany joked. "How am I going to face him next Sunday?"

They burst out in laughter as they caught up with the two children and proceeded to the Barry home. The two-story traditional had a wraparound porch, which held a wicker rocker and a two-seat porch swing. The large skeleton was sprawled in an incline position on the swing, emitting a guttural laughing sound on a loop.

Brenda took the steps two at a time, reaching the top with a bounce. Her mind previously focused on candy bars, but she stopped short when she heard the sound. A strange howling noise came from under the house. Frightened, she turned and ran back to her mother, who had been waiting with her friend at the bottom of the steps.

"Bren?" Tiffany looked down into the frightened face of her little girl. "You didn't knock on the door."

Brenda's breath came in gasps. "Mommy! I heard a monster in the house."

Tiffany let out a throaty laugh. "Oh, Honey, it's Halloween! Ms. Barry probably has that spooky CD you wanted us to buy at the party store. Let's go tell Ms. Barry to turn it down a bit."

When they got to the porch, Tiffany heard it. There was a high-pitched howling coming from somewhere below them. Was it an injured animal? She felt the hair rise on the back of her neck.

"What the hell is that?" Beth had heard it as well.

Knocking loudly on the door, Tiffany started calling out to Ms. Barry. "Martha? Martha? Are you all right? It's Tiffany?"

The porch light went off, and the entire house went dark. It was as if the house, so magically animated seconds before, had suddenly died. They heard the howling sound once more before it was stopped suddenly following a crash.

Tiffany Place felt the beginnings of panic rising in her own throat. She was sure she had just heard the sound of someone being hurt. Taking Brenda by the hand, Tiffany started down the stairs. Beth followed closely behind.

"Let's go right now, Brenda."

Tiffany bid her friend goodbye and did not let go of her daughter's hand until they were safely back inside their own home. The warm quiet of their kitchen soothed her frazzled nerves. She dumped Brenda's treat back on the kitchen table and instructed the little girl to pick out five pieces she could have that night.

Happy with the prospect of eating that much candy, Brenda busied herself with the task, forgetting the noises they had heard at the Barry house.

Tiffany walked into the dining room, quietly closing the door that separated that room from the kitchen. She leaned against the wall and took a deep breath until her hands stopped shaking. She then picked up her cell phone and dialed 911.

When the operator answered, Brenda explained the sounds she had heard coming from the basement. She had been afraid that someone had broken into the house and injured Ms. Barry. Or worse.

The operator assured the frightened woman that a car would be dispatched immediately.

Relieved, Tiffany re-entered the kitchen in time to see Brenda sneak a miniature Snickers bar into her mouth. Smiling at the sight of her chocolate-faced princess, Brenda sat at the table and helped the child sort candy.

10

The Boy

He stirred and moaned softly. The pain in his head was worse than he had ever felt. It was even colder than usual, and all the light had left the room. As he tried to sit up, he bumped his head. Frantically, his hands moved above, below, and to his side. Panic choked his breath as the reality set in. He was in the freezer.

Try as he might to move the heavy lid, it would not budge. The panic rose and became so real that he thought his heart would stop. He couldn't breathe, and his head hurt so badly he thought he would throw up again.

She's just mad cause I yelled. She'll come soon and let me out. I have to say I'm sorry.

But he couldn't think of what he'd say to her. His head hurt so bad; all he could do was pray.

Momma used to make him say his prayers every night. She would tell him that bad things happened to little boys who forgot to pray. It had been a long time since he had talked to anyone, much less God.

Maybe God's forgotten me, too.

As he tried to remember how to say a prayer, a new feeling came over him very slowly. It wasn't so cold now. He was gonna be okay. He wasn't even scared anymore; in fact, he was very sleepy.

Yes, I'll just go to sleep.

He began to drift off when he heard new voices. They sounded like they were in the basement, but he just kept quiet. He felt warm and happy now, and sleep welcomed him with a hug.

11

Jennifer

The iPhone vibrated loudly, jarring Jennifer into consciousness. She sat up with a start.

"Oh, My God." she exclaimed when she glanced at the clock face of the phone. It was almost 6:00 pm. Why hadn't the damn alarm gone off?

When the phone buzzed again, she snatched it up and tersely answered. "Jennifer Riley."

There was silence initially. Then a voice asked tentatively, "Jennifer?" she heard Michael's voice. "Did I catch you at a bad time?"

Jennifer figuratively kicked herself for the tone and adjusted her voice.

"Yes, Michael, I am fine. I ran home to grab a bite and fell asleep on the couch. I'm just mad at myself. I have to get moving and run back to the office. Those records are not going to read themselves, you know."

"Well, I hate to bother you, but we got a bad one."

"You mean the Ossie case? Yeah, I know. I sent Daniel out on it this morning. I didn't bother you because I knew you were finishing up on your cases." She didn't want to tell him that the truth of the matter was that she didn't think he was ready for a child death case.

"No, not the Ossie case. I heard about that one in the unit."

"What are you talking about?" Jennifer felt herself becoming irritated and knew she needed to be more patient.

Michael explained to her that he had been closing up his computer when he heard the intake line ring. The intake line was supposed to be switched to the on-call unit phone after 4:00 pm, but he realized someone had forgotten to switch it.

He took the call, which turned out to be a serious case that required an immediate response.

"I didn't want to send out the on-call person because it would just come back to the serious abuse unit. And I was supposed to be on emergency today, so I figured the call was Karma's way of saying, 'batter up.'"

She heard him laugh good-naturedly at his own joke and thought again about how much she admired the young investigator. Most workers would be thrilled that they did not get called out on an emergency and wouldn't have volunteered to handle one after hours.

"Thanks, Michael, I appreciate that. So tell me about the case."

"We don't have much to go on right now. MPD called intake. Some trick-or-treater heard a scream coming from the basement of an older home and called them. The caller thought the adult female in the home was being assaulted."

"Why didn't they call the adult unit?" Jennifer asked.

"Turns out it wasn't an adult. It was a bizarre situation. When BPD arrived, the lady was fine but didn't want to let them into the house. They would have just left then, but her behavior became so bizarre that they questioned her about who else was in the house."

"Bizarre how?"

"Apparently, she started cursing in one breath and praying for God to strike them dead in the other. She kept saying that they could NOT go into the basement because a demon lived there."

"Wow," Jennifer said. "So let me guess. Since the screams came from the basement and the lady seemed fine, they went into the basement."

"Yep. Corporal James told me that with her erratic behavior and the neighbors' claim that they heard someone being harmed, the police felt that they had probable cause to enter the house and search the basement."

"Michael, tell me there wasn't a dead body or something like that."

"Well, not quite. Apparently, she ran past them, threw herself across an old deep freezer, and began crying about hiding the demon. When they opened the freezer, they found a small boy inside."

"What? A child? In the freezer?"

"Jennifer, he was unconscious and almost dead."

"Jeez!" Jennifer exclaimed. "How horrible for that poor child. Yes, it is a bad one. Do you want me to go out with you? Sounds like this will be a high-profile situation."

"No, I can handle it. Right now, the boy is at the ER over at the University of South Alabama Hospital. He's still unconscious, but they are working on him. The lady (I am guessing mom, but we really don't know) was taken to Mobile Infirmary in a catatonic state. She's likely to be admitted to the Psych Ward. I am going to the neighbor's house first and get some background. Both the kid and the mom can't be interviewed right now."

Jennifer admitted it was a good plan of action. "Let me know if I can help any."

"If I need you, you know I will give you a shout! Officer Jordan with MPD was working with Corporal James and told me he would look into Crazy Mom's background and see if there are any priors."

Jennifer pursed her lips. She did not like it when her staff called parents crazy. That did not meet their mission of getting to the underlying issues with families without labeling. But she had to admit that locking your child in a freezer probably qualified for the mentally ill label.

"Okay, Michael, I am coming to the office to close out the month. God knows I will probably be there until 10 or 11. Please call me when you have any more information."

"I will do that, Jennifer." Before the line was disconnected, she heard him mutter, "I hate Halloween."

Replacing the cell into her purse and rushing toward the door, she agreed, "Me too."

At the office, Jennifer headed straight to her mailbox. As she had suspected, ten cases were waiting to be reviewed for closure. According to her tracking log, those ten made up the last cases due for October. Gratified that her unit had worked hard to get them all in, she now had the responsibility to review and close them out. She sighed loudly. Her words to Michael had been predictive. It would be a long night.

Jennifer had glimpsed Daniel sitting at his desk when she walked onto the unit but hadn't spoken to him. He looked so busy entering data onto his laptop that she hadn't wanted to stop his progress. She guessed that he was entering notes on the case from today because Daniel prided himself on entering his narratives on the day he gathered them.

From her cursory glance of the unit, she surmised that she and Daniel were not the only ones still on the floor. Her workers had learned that, on the last day of the month, it was wiser to remain close by until she had reviewed all their reports in case corrections were needed. But her little nap had thrown them all behind, and she felt terrible for them. She knew the staff had planned a Halloween party at one of the local bars. Determined to knock out the reviews quickly, she grabbed a folder and dug in.

Three cases later, Jennifer sat back in her desk chair, the hinge squeak sounding like a bullet in the quiet room. She called Kim.

"Hey, Jennifer, You done with my cases?"

"I am. And you did a really good job, especially on the Gutierrez one. The collateral check with the adult children turned out to be very revealing."

Kim chuckled. "Yes, Ma'am, thanks. It is always a hoot what you can learn from the kiddos who got on out of the situation."

"Well, as I said, particularly good work. All of yours are complete and closed off the system. Go have fun!"

"I plan to! Bucky said he would take me to the CPS Halloween party. He is just waitin' at home for me. We are going as a Gomez and Morticia because he wants to flaunt his new mustache."

"I think you guys will be cute," Jennifer said. "Go! Enjoy! I have to get back to reading records."

Jennifer picked up Michael's last record as Kim left the office. But before she could open it, the phone rang. The caller ID announced it was him calling.

"Hi, Michael."

Michael jumped right into the narrative. "I spoke with Tiffany Place, the woman who contacted the police. She knew a lot about this family. But she didn't know that the little boy still lived there."

"Where did she think he lived?"

"The back story is this. The house belonged to Ken and Martha Barry. They lived there for several years with their two sons, Billy and Christopher. Billy was killed several months ago while playing baseball. Listen to this. Lightning struck him."

"What? How the hell does a little boy get hit by lightning? How awful!"

"Right? A quick storm blew up while they were playing, and before the coach could get the kids off the field, a stray bolt of lightning hit Billy, and he died."

Jennifer drew in a sharp breath. She could not imagine how horrible it would be to watch your child die like that. But she remained silent as Michael continued.

"Mrs. Barry had a breakdown after that and had to be hospitalized. Ms. Place wasn't sure what hospital. She thought it had just been all too much for the husband because he mysteriously left town shortly afterward. No one in the neighborhood had seen Chris since the accident, so everyone assumed Mr. Barry had taken Chris with him."

"And is the boy in the hospital, Chris?"

"We assume so," answered Michael. "He appears to be the right age. But there is no record that the child attended school this year. Plus, the little tyke in the hospital is still unconscious, so we can't ask.

"Is there anything else that Mrs. Place could tell you?"

Michael added, "She said that the mother was always a little "bipolar."

"Bipolar was her word?"

"Michael laughed. "Yes. Ms. Place is a counselor at the Mental Health Center. She described Mrs. Barry as ultra-manic most of the time. She kept the house and the yard spotless and the children immaculate. Full of energy, Mrs. Barry would volunteer for every neighborhood sale, event, and task. The consensus is she was generally well-liked. But, according to the neighbor, other times, Mrs. Barry would swing toward depression and not get out of bed for days."

Jennifer processed the information before asking, "Did she have any other information on the boy?"

"She had always observed that Mrs. Barry was extremely attached to Chris. Her exact words were that mom kept him tied to her apron strings. The gossip on the block was that he was autistic or 'special' in some way. But she did not know this to be true."

Jennifer paused. "Okay," Michael, that's all good information. Go over to the hospital and check in on Chris to see if that is who he is. Ask the doctor about his prognosis and if they can tell if he has been abused long term."

"I'm on my way now. I will let you know if he is awake or if I can get anything from the doctor."

"Sounds good. After you see the little boy, go home. I am finishing up your last case for review and don't see any issues with it."

"I will. I am all curious now to see if the boy is Chris. So I am on the way to USA. Talk to you soon."

As she replaced the cradle, Jennifer processed Michael's call. While there was not much information yet, her heart went out to this boy who had lost so much in the span of a few months: his brother, his father, his freedom, and almost his life. Cases like this made her long for the days when she investigated rather than supervised. There are so many avenues she would want to pursue.

Why had the mother imprisoned her son? Where had the father gone, and why did he leave his little boy? Where was the extended family? Why did the neighbors not think to call sooner? The not knowing was sometimes more burdensome than the knowing.

Although she had been thinking about little Chris, the face that came to Jennifer's mind was not his. It was Candy's face. Her chest tightened as her thoughts turned to today's service. She had heard about Candy almost as an aside. She might never have known if Detective Green had not been the investigator.

The regrets inched their way into her mind. Candy shouldn't have died! Candy should have called her if things were going badly. She loved her job, but it always felt like she was getting to the action too late. Why couldn't they get called before the bad things happened? How could she make a difference if she didn't know until it was too late?

Her fingers brushed at the auburn bangs that covered her eyes, and she felt the moisture on her fingertips. She mentally berated herself for giving in to whatever this was: self-pity, grief, exhaustion. The tears, however, began to flow slowly.

"Hey, boss-lady, here is the…"

Daniel's voice trailed off as he took in her wet cheeks. "What happened?"

Startled, she flushed as if she had been caught naked. Embarrassed, she quickly wiped her eyes with the back of her hand, took a long breath in, and then steeled herself to calm.

"Um," she began and gave a quick snort that was a failed attempt at a laugh. Then she noticed the look of concern in his eyes and sighed. "Look, this has just been a very long week that is catching up with me."

Daniel saw the tiredness in her eyes, but fatigue was not the underlying emotion he observed. Jennifer had worked longer hours than this without batting an eye. No, not this was not just exhaustion. He admired her strong boundaries and decided she would tell him when she wanted him to know.

More curious to him was his own reaction to her sadness. This vulnerable side of her, which had remained hidden before now, touched him, fueling a desire to understand. He wanted to draw close to her, get her to open up to him, and let him into her world. And, he had to admit, he wanted to take away some of her pain.

Daniel acknowledged her physical beauty, but it was her analytical brain, her irreverent sense of humor, and her incredible inner strength that attracted him to her. Now, seeing yet another facet of the woman before him, stirred a place in his heart that he had thought long dead.

What was he thinking? She was right to put up such boundaries. Office romances were complex enough, but this dynamic could become overly complicated. No, Daniel. Forget it.

Daniel nodded and said, "Sometimes, it's all just a little too much, isn't it? I know. I have been there myself."

When he did not push, the gratitude in her eyes made him want to help her all the more. Instead, he just smiled and changed the subject: "I came in here to update you on the Ossie case."

The weak smile she aimed his way disappeared. "What is the baby's prognosis?"

Daniel shook his head. The doctor said the baby would not last the night. Tomorrow, this will be a child death case."

Her hand slammed down, creating a muffled clack on the hollow wood of her desk. "You know, Daniel, I am sick and damned tired of people killing their children."

The forcefulness of her action took Daniel aback. "Well, yes, so are we all. But you were always the cheerleader for not passing judgment until all the facts were in play. Are you sure you are okay?"

"I told you, Daniel," she snapped, instantly wishing she had not. "I am fine. Are you any closer to figuring out who shook that baby?"

Daniel eyed her thoughtfully, continuing, "My money is on the boyfriend. I just have to dig up the proof."

Jennifer reminded him. "Our priority is ensuring the safety of the other children. Did Kim pick up Jason and put him in care?

"Yes, this afternoon. The kid didn't even put up a fuss. If that doesn't tell you something about his attachment issues, nothing will."

"Daniel, thank you for making sure he was safe. We can't let him go home until Mom can demonstrate that she has protective capacities. And we just don't know enough yet to say that."

Daniel agreed. "I know that in her current state, she has not demonstrated the ability to protect, even if she did not kill the baby. Knowing her partner's propensity for violence and yet allowing him to be alone with her child says a lot about her own internal issues and family history."

"The cycle continues until someone breaks it," Jennifer said quietly, almost to herself. "Just today, we have dealt with two separate cases where women seemed to have broken free and gotten their lives together only to fall back into familiar patterns which ended in tragedy."

Understanding lightened Daniel's gaze. He approached the topic carefully. "That's right. You went to the funeral of a foster child today. That is why you were crying."

Jennifer looked away without answering, but Daniel continued. "Seems surreal, doesn't it? You worked closely with her for so long., and she responded to your interventions. She started making a positive life change. She was a success."

"How do you know all of that?" Jennifer looked confused. I didn't tell you that. You didn't know Candy."

"No, I didn't know Candy. But I have been there. My foster child was Paul. He ran away from an abusive situation as well when he was thirteen. It's a long story, but the end result is that despite all that he wanted to grab out of life, he grabbed some bad drugs instead and OD'ed. Made me sick."

"Exactly! I believed Candy was going to be happy, successful, and, most of all, safe. But look what happened to her? Was I wrong? Did I miss an underlying issue we could have addressed that would have made her stronger? Could I have foreseen that this boyfriend, she talked about all the time, had the same traits as her father? I should have met him. Would I have been able to see it then? Why didn't she tell me when things started to go south?"

"Jennifer," Daniel's voice softened. "We have to mourn the hurt and acknowledge the pain when it comes that close to us. Most of us long-timers have been in your shoes. If you work in CPS long enough, you can't avoid it. But what we cannot do is take the blame."

Jennifer sniffed. "Who is to blame then?"

"The only one who is to blame for Candy's death is the bastard who killed her. Candy may not have seen it coming, either. She chose to be with the dude. The people we work with, the ones we try to help, have the right to make choices, even if we don't understand them."

"So, we do nothing?" Jennifer knew everything Daniel said was true but just felt like she had to argue.

"We can listen to them when they call. We can guide them through healing when they ask. But in the end, we are all affected by the choices we make. Even Candy."

"We have so few successes in this job," Jennifer echoed. "Sometimes I wonder why we keep doing it."

"Because those few are enough," he said softly.

At first, Jennifer just stared at him. Daniel wondered if he had gone too far and pushed too hard. Then her shoulders relaxed, and the walls came back up.

"Daniel, I am sorry you had to see me like this. Believe me, it doesn't happen often. But you are right. Everything I am handling today is shadowed by my grief for Candy."

"I get it. It can just be too much sometimes."

"You're right, Danial. I know you're telling me the hard truth, but I need to hear it again sometimes. I'll get up tomorrow and keep swimming. Because no matter how upset I am today, in the big picture, I believe in what we do."

"But," she looked at him in mock fierceness, "if you keep standing here running your mouth when I have reports to read, neither of us will be going home tonight."

When she smiled, Daniel could see that the air had lightened. "That's my supervisor."

Jennifer waved her arm toward him. "Go on! Get out of my office and let me do my job so I can go home."

With an exaggerated salute, he turned to leave. "Yes, Ma'am. Night Boss."

"Daniel?" he stopped as she called out his name. He turned to face her and was struck again by how pretty she looked. Jennifer Riley was pretty. No, more than that. She was beautiful. He hardly had time to figure out why he was thinking such thoughts when he heard her say, "Thank you. For listening. For understanding."

He shrugged. "Just remember all that at my evaluation time."

"Get out," she laughed.

Alone with her thoughts, Jennifer admitted to herself that she had been a little surprised but strangely comforted to find that Daniel had such in-depth knowledge about trauma and pain. She wondered if he had learned it from the job or from a personal experience. It didn't matter. She didn't have time to think about things like that. If she ever wanted to go home, she had to finish up the last of the reviews.

An hour later, Jennifer completed the final case review. With a weary sigh, she grabbed her purse and headed home. Her thoughts circled around Daniel. She had felt drawn to him this evening, wishing they could have gone out and grabbed a drink. There was no use thinking about useless things like that. Relationships between supervisor and their staff were strictly forbidden at DHR. Besides, she had never picked up on any vibe that he would even be interested in her.

Shifting her mind to a late dinner, she decided to stop by McAllister's and pick up a Vegetable baked potato. As she passed the security guard's desk, she spied a bowl of Halloween candy and scooped up a handful.

Winking at the security guard, she proclaimed, "Dessert!"

12

Jennifer

On the drive back to her apartment, Jennifer realized she had not spoken with Michael after sending him to the hospital. She already felt angry at herself, and embarrassed for displaying such vulnerability around Daniel, and now she just forgot about one of her staff working late in the field. Requesting Siri call his cell, she heard him answer on the first ring.

"Michael. Sounds like you are driving. I hope that means you're heading home. Can you give me a quick update on your emergency?"

"Sorry, Jennifer," she heard. "I planned to call you when I got to the house."

"Fret Not," she joked. "It's been one of those days. Do you want to call me back?"

"No. I have hands-free, so I can update you now. The boy has not woken up yet but is in a regular room now."

"Thank goodness," breathed Jennifer. "What's his prognosis?"

"I got the chance to talk to Dr. Crumb, who said that the child was severely dehydrated and underweight. Plus, there were old and new scars, like from a belt or an extension cord, which show he had been severely whipped on more than one occasion."

"Can they tell when he was last whipped?"

"Not definitively. I had hoped to get his name at least to make sure it was Chris. But while the boy regained consciousness briefly in the E.R., which was great news to the doctor, he immediately fell unconscious again. He is on some heavy meds right now, but the prognosis is good, and the doc said I could come by tomorrow when the kid will be more awake."

"And the screaming that the neighbor heard. If Mom was upstairs, who was hurting him?" she did not like mysteries.

"That is the other piece I wanted to tell you. He was poisoned. Someone, presumably his mother, gave him something, maybe to keep him quiet while people came over, and his body reacted with it."

"Poisoned? Do they know what she used?"

Michael interjected, "They ran a tox screen and will know something in a couple of weeks. They pumped his stomach, and he's resting. Dr. Crump thinks mom just gave him something she had on hand."

"All so she could enjoy Halloween with no interruptions. I have no words."

"I know, right? But the bottom line is, apart from the headache and gastrointestinal distress, the child suffered no severe damage as a result of the drugs."

Jennifer was relieved. "That is some good news, at least. What about other indicators of past abuse?"

"Doc said there were some scars, scrapes, scratches, and a few yellowing bruises, but no broken bones or anything. The extension cord marks I mentioned vary in age from a couple of months ago to as recently as a week ago."

Jennifer sighed. "Poor thing. Okay, good work, Michael. We know a lot more than we did a couple of hours ago. So where do we go from here?"

She heard Michael laugh. "Isn't that what I am supposed to ask you?"

"I was thinking out loud, funny man, talking to myself," she said. "Tomorrow, we'll need to talk to the boy and the mom if she is verbal. We need to find Dad as well. How about we split this up? You're so good with the kids, Michael. You take the boy. Did we ever find out for sure it was Chris?"

"Yes, I asked Ms. Place to come to the emergency room. She identified the little boy as Christopher Barry. They called him Chris."

"Okay, you take Chris, and I will try to interview the mom. Is she still at Mobile Infirmary?"

"Yes, on the psych ward. Honestly, I haven't even checked to see if she can have visitors yet."

"I know some people there," Jennifer said. "I will see if I can get an interview. This is a complicated situation, Michael. And it will be a lot more complex than your other previously investigated cases. You need to let me know when you need help."

"You are interviewing the mom, which will be extremely helpful, and it will give me time to try and find dad. So, thanks! Sounds like a plan, supervisor. See you tomorrow."

Jennifer added, "Thanks again, Michael, for taking this one. I think it was meant for you."

When she reached her apartment, Jennifer gathered her purse and exited the car. She noticed that the temperature had fallen a bit since even earlier that evening. Yes, a crisp wind danced around her face as she walked, bringing with it the thought, "Fall is finally coming to the South."

13

Chris
Chris Barry opened his eyes slowly, wincing at the brightness of the light. Everything was white. He wondered if he was dead. And if he was, would he see Billy? The thought did not scare him at all. He found relief in the prospect of seeing his brother again.

Chris tried to remember what happened. He remembered screaming in pain from his tummy and his head. He didn't mean to make her mad, but it hurt so much! The memory from the previous night slowly inched into his consciousness. Momma must have heard him because she ran down the stairs with a look so fierce that he wet his pants.

After that, everything went blank.

His eyes adjusted to the brightness, and other things became focused. And he heard the sounds of people talking in a low voice. The voices were not familiar, so he kept his eyes shut. A steady beeping came from near him, but he didn't know what that was either. That awful pain that had been in his head and in his belly had mostly gone away, but he felt stiff and sore. And he smelled; he smelled clean. He wasn't sure how he remembered what clean smelled like, but it was nice.

The puzzle pieces worked together in his head and Chris figured out that he must be in a hospital. It was his first time in a hospital as a sick person. But Billy had gone to a hospital one time to get his tonsils taken out. Chris got to visit his brother during that trip. Billy kept bragging that he was lucky to be in the hospital because of all the ice cream he got to eat!

A nurse stood next to the bed, fidgeting with a long pole. She didn't know he was awake, so he watched her curiously. She had light brown skin and short hair. With long eyelashes and an upturned nose, Chris thought she was beautiful. The song she hummed was strange, but the sound was nice, and it relaxed him. He studied the pole and the bag of water or something hanging from a hook at the top. It seemed to be dripping into a tube that ran down the pole over to the bed and into his arm. He wasn't scared, but he was curious and wondered why it didn't hurt his arm to have that stuff coming into it.

A squeaking sound, like wheels that needed a good grease job, came from the hallway as another lady rolled past the door, pushing a big cart full of food trays.

He heard the pretty nurse say, "Don't bother leaving the tray; he's not awake."

Jerking his head around to protest, he caught her looking right at him with a smile in her eyes. She had known. He answered anyway. "Yes, I am. I'm awake."

She acted surprised. "Well, so you are. I think you were playing possum on me. Is that what you were doing?"

He looked at her sheepishly but did not answer."

"I guess, if you are for sure awake, you might want some breakfast then."

"I am for sure awake."

She took the tray from the other nurse and placed it on a weird-looking table that had little wheels on the legs. With one hand, she plumped up his pillows and, with the other, pushed a button that made his bed raise up at the head. He felt himself sitting up without even trying. She moved the rolling table until the tray was over his bed right in front of him. Just like that! And all the while she was doing these things, she was talking to him.

"My name is Karen. I am your nurse all day today. So if you need anything, you just push this button right here." She moved a large box-like thing, some TV remote, next to him with buttons on it. She explained to him which ones turned on the TV, which adjusted the volume, and which button called for the nurse.

He listened intently to her instructions, quite sure he needed to know these important things.

"Now, I will ask you a silly question, but I need you to answer me. Do you know what your name is?"

He was quiet for a few seconds. He appeared to be thinking very hard. Then, a smile spread across his face. "My name is Christopher Earl Barry. People call me Chris."

"Very nice to meet you, Chris." She lifted the round silver cover on the plate and said, "Ta-Da!"

At first, the boy just stared at the food.

Karen quickly explained, "Now I know this is not an overly exciting breakfast. No bacon, sausages, or Salsa! But the doctor, well, he could tell when you came in that you haven't been eating a whole lot lately."

He stared at her silently, not knowing what to say.

She never stopped. Well, Chris, when you don't eat for a long time, your tummy gets smaller and a little pickier about what kind of food it will let you eat. No spicy food, not a great deal of food at one time. You understand?"

Chris shook his head. "No, if I am really hungry, why can't I eat a lot of food?"

Karen smiled. Because your tummy thinks you want a lot of food, but once it gets some food inside, it will get full so fast. Because remember, it got smaller. So, if you eat too much or food that upsets your tummy, it'll make a rumble. You don't want that, do you?"

Wide-eyed, the boy shook his head back and forth quickly. He remembered the pain from the day before.

The nurse busied herself, opening the milk carton and pouring it into the small cup.

Chris looked at the tray. He saw the scrambled eggs, grits, toast, and milk. As if on sheer instinct, he grabbed up a handful of the eggs and stuffed them into his mouth.

She gently touched his hand. He snatched it back immediately, fearful of what she would do. Had he already broken the rules? Would he be punished?

But instead, she patted his hand and said, "Here, Chris, let me help you."

Karen picked up the napkin and wiped his mouth, but egg bits were still on his lips. "I know you haven't eaten regularly in a long time, and you just want to grab it up before it disappears. Or before I take it all away. You know what, I would want to do the same thing."

He stared at her.

How did she know what he was thinking?

"But I promise you, Sweetie, this food is going nowhere. And I will make sure you get every single bite if you will let me help." She picked up a spoon, dipped it into the buttery grits, and brought the spoon to his lips. He sipped greedily. Oh, how wonderful it felt going down his throat, warm and delicious. She gave him a bite of bread with jam to chew and it was so soft and sweet. As she fed him, she kept on talking. And the sound of her voice made him happy.

"By the way," her tone remained soft and calm. "Your social worker came in bright and early this morning to see you. He had to step out into the hall a few minutes ago to make a call, but he will be so excited to see you awake and doing so good."

"What's a social worker?" he had been chewing on the egg when he spoke, and pieces of yellow and white gooeyness flew out of his mouth and onto the tray. She patiently picked up the errant pieces and wiped his mouth again with the napkin. He took a drink of milk, swallowed, and then stopped suddenly, looking alarmed.

"Where's my mom? Is she here?" as he spoke those words his heart began to beat faster. Soon the thing was pounding in his chest. He felt fear creep back over his body covering him with an icy coat. Karen noticed the change and ran her fingers gently through his hair.

"Oh, child," she whispered. "It's okay. Your mother's not here. You are safe." Her fingers smoothed back his hair in a regular soothing motion as she talked. She could not imagine what this child had been through to be this skinny and almost dead from hyperthermia. As Karen continued to stroke his hair and repeat that he was safe, she could feel him visibly unclench.

"Social Worker?" Chris asked again.

Karen nodded. "Right. A social worker is someone who works with kids who come from scary or hurtful situations. He helps make them safe. Michael is your worker, and he is very nice."

"How do you know he is nice," suspicion in the young voice.

"Because I have worked with him before. And he was able to keep another little boy safe."

"Michael," repeated Chris. "How can he keep me safe?"

"Oh," Karen obviously wasn't prepared for the question. "Well, for one, he will find a nice family to take care of you. And also… well… um… Anyway, I'm sure he will tell you all about that when he comes back. I don't want to spoil his fun. You go ahead and finish your breakfast, and he will be here soon."

Chris ate another bite of the eggs and grits, but then, to his own astonishment, he pushed the plate away. "I'm full."

"I'm not surprised. Remember how I told you that when you don't eat much for a long time, your stomach gets smaller? In just a little while, after eating regular meals, your stomach will expand, and you can eat more."

Before Chris could respond, he heard a male voice.

"I see our boy is awake and eating up all the grits!"

A tall black man wearing brown pants and a loosely fitting red sweater entered the room. Chris knew it had to be the social worker because he didn't know anyone else. Karen introduced the man as

Michael and then updated the social worker on the morning's events. She rolled away the table and the half-eaten tray of food with it.

Michael asked Karen about the new hospital cook, and he began laughing as the pretty nurse made an exaggerated gesture of throwing up. Chris watched their interchange and decided the guy might be okay.

Pulling a chair next to the bed, Michael flashed a toothy grin at the small boy. When he spoke, his voice was soft and calm.

"Chris, I am so happy to finally meet you. As you may have guessed, I'm Michael. You, my new friend, are so important that someone decided that you should get your very own social worker!"

Chris eyed the man without speaking.

"Hmmm, I don't think you are nearly as excited to see me as I am to see you," joked Michael. "Maybe I should start over." He cleared his throat and straightened his collar. Extending his hand, he said, "Pleased to meet you. I am your social worker. Do you know what a social worker is?"

Chris ignored the outstretched hand. He didn't want to be rude, but he wasn't sure what to make of this guy. He offered a tentative smile. "You are supposed to keep me safe and find a family to take care of me."

Michael laughed heartily and said, "I should have known Karen would fill you in. She does like to talk, doesn't she?" He gave the nurse a wink before turning back to Chris. "Yes, I am definitely going to do those things. As a matter of fact, I was just on the phone with a foster parent while you were eating up all the breakfast. I wanted to make sure they would be a good fit for you."

Chris felt cold anxiety rising. "My momma said no one would ever want to take me in. What if you cannot find a fit for me?"

Michael reached out again, and this time, he took the boy's small hand into his. "Don't you worry about that, Chris? I already have a family that is dying to meet you and take you into their family until we sort everything out."

"Really? You told them about me, and they said they want me?"

"Want you? They feel lucky that you might want them! Their names are Mr. and Mrs. Guidry, and they have a son named Devon, who is twelve years old. How old are you, Chris? Eighteen? Nineteen?"

Chris rolled his eyes but enjoyed the joke. "No! I am nine years old."

Karen, who had remained near, clicked her tongue. She would have guessed closer to six if she had to guess by his size.

Michael continued, "Well, you will have a big brother then. How would you like that?"

Chris' smile faltered, and his eyes began to water. Michael mentally kicked himself for not thinking!

Karen came over when she noticed the boy's distress. "What is it, Child?" she asked softly, ignoring Michael's quick shake of the head.

"I already used to have a big brother," he began.

"Where is he now?" asked Karen.

"He is in heaven." And the boy began to weep softly.

Michael got closer and put his arm around the boy's shoulders. He had known about the death of Chris' brother earlier in the year and realized the pain of unresolved grief. There was so much information he would need from Chris to put together all the pieces of the puzzle: how the family fell apart and how he came to be in his current condition. But that could wait for now. This morning, Michael just wanted Chris to feel safe.

*****

Jennifer had been sitting at her desk for almost an hour when she heard the sharp rap at the open door. She looked up and smiled when she saw Daniel holding two Starbucks cups.

"Fantastic! How did you guess I was caffeine deficient?" she bantered.

Laying the black-lidded cup on her desk, he took a quick swig of his own. "I just figured you stayed here late last night to finish up the records and might could use a jolt of java."

She paused to breathe in the dark aroma of the coffee. The smell reminded her of her daddy. After her mother died, she lived with him while she finished up at school. He was supposed to take care of her, but they ended up taking care of each other. The smell memory was so strong because for the entire year she was there, every morning, he would make a pot of coffee with chicory, dark and strong. He used to say, "If you have to doctor it up well, it's not coffee anymore." She opened the lid, blew on the surface, and then took a sip. "Mmm. Good," she mumbled.

Noticing Daniel's amused eyes, she added, "Sorry. I was having a moment. Uh, what were we talking about?" Then she quickly added, "Oh, yeah, I finished reading and closed all of the cases out of the system."

"What time did you head out?"

"I actually didn't leave much after you. Once you stopped talking and I could concentrate, the work went pretty fast."

Daniel was still smiling. "Well, I will just take away my coffee there; you probably don't need it."

She snatched her hand back. "Don't you dare!"

He raised his hands in the air. "Fine. While you're enjoying your Java, let me update you on the Ossie case."

Jennifer waved him on as she sipped.

"It's not good news. Little Carrie passed away early this morning. Mom was with her when she died but was then transported to the police station for questioning."

Jennifer shook her head. "That is so awful, Daniel. Did you get an idea who shook the baby? They did decide it was shaken baby, right?"

Daniel nodded and referred to his notes. "Traumatic Brain Injury caused by violent shaking of the infant. However, we still do not have solid evidence of who shook the baby. Neither mom nor the boyfriend is implicating the other, and both deny the act."

"Of course,"

"Mom presents as devastated, and I am sure she is, but that doesn't rule her out as the Perpetrator."

"Where are you on your collaterals?"

"I still have to go interview the neighbor, Miss Katz. She's the one Ms. Ossie said kept Carrie while she was out with Brian, the boyfriend. I will need that corroboration."

Listening intently, Jennifer nodded her head. "Unfortunately, unless you find something that definitively implicates one or the other for the shaking, you will not be able to indicate either."

Daniel's eyes flashed, "I want to indicate them both! They are both responsible! The one who didn't actually shake the baby is covering for the one who did!"?

She knew that frustration. "Well, Daniel, you're the best investigator I have. If there is evidence to find, you'll find it. Go out and talk to the neighbor. She may give you something more than just corroboration. You know how neighbors seem to know more than they let on. And if you can't point to just one, go ahead and indicate them both. I will stand behind you at the due process review. Document so well that they cannot possibly overturn it."

"Thanks, Jennifer."

She added, "Make sure to get a solid timeline of their movements from the previous night until they brought the child in. Talk to everyone they saw. Maybe we can narrow it down and prove only one of them was with the child when it happened."

Daniel held up his notebook. "Great Minds!"

Jennifer saw he had written across the page in bold ink: *MAKE A TIMELINE.* TALK TO EVERYONE

She smiled and said, "See how superfluous I am? You don't need me at all."

He protested. "No, we might have to fight the administrative review together, so it is good that we are on the same page. Jason, her other child, is with Mrs. Boyd, and she is a great foster parent, so he will be safe."

"Does he know that his little sister passed away?" Jennifer asked.

"I called Ms. Boyd. She will take Jason to play therapy today so that when he is told, he can express his feelings. You know he didn't just lose a sister; he lost his entire family."

"That will leave an emotional scar for sure."

Silence filled the room as both considered the grief of a six-year-old child who had lost everything.

Daniel rose. "I am leaving in a few to go to Miss Katz's house. I will let you know how it goes with her." He turned to leave the office but looked back and saw Jennifer drinking deeply of the coffee with her eyes closed.

With frustration, Jennifer glanced at the growing stack of red folders in her basket. She and her team had worked hard to complete all the October due cases by the end of the month, but they just kept on coming. She knew she would have new cases to assign as long as adults took out their stress and anger on children.

Jennifer grabbed a folder and began reading through the narrative when she noticed the red message light blinking on her phone. Wondering when it had been left, she pushed the retrieval button. Michael had called in early that morning to alert her that he would be stopping by the hospital to check on Chris before heading into the office.

She jotted a quick note on her sticky pad to "Call Michael about basement boy." Someone not in this business would be horrified by her description on the note. But the truth was that there were so many cases coming through each week that until she got to know the cases and the situations better, she learned to assign the case a description that would help her delineate it from the others. Once she became more familiar with the case, she would remember the case name and all the participants.

Daniel's Ossie case had been a bit different because, in a child death case, she had to prepare multiple reports to the state office, the DA, and the child death review team so that she was unlikely to forget that name.

Suddenly remembering her conversation with the State Office that morning, she contacted Daniel again.

"Yes, Jennifer?"

"I forgot to tell you that the State Office wants a timeline by 3. We only just talked about it this morning, so if you need some more time, let me know."

"Yeah. I don't think I will have it by three. I am on my way to Mrs. Katz now; then I want to track down Bryan and the meth buddies. Not that I think they will be forthcoming, but they will be instrumental in the timeline."

Jennifer paused briefly before replying, "Get it to me by noon tomorrow, and I will let the State Office know what we are facing with this. Thanks, Daniel. Check back in with me this evening with what you find today."

"Will do," Daniel signed off.

As she hung up the phone, she thought he had sounded a little cold and business-like, which was out of character for him. It was probably just her imagination. Hadn't he brought her coffee? And besides, why would she even care? She was his supervisor, and it shouldn't matter. Jennifer made another sticky note to check in with Kim on the Bicycle helmet case, and then she went back to reading and assigning new reports.

By 10:00 am, she had reviewed the three new pending investigations, checked their history, and assigned each one to an investigator.

The last report of the morning was one of domestic violence where the mother's boyfriend had threatened her with a gun in front of the children. The police were able to break it up, but the children were traumatized. And looking at the history, this was the second boyfriend of that mother who had hurt her in front of her children.

How would they ever learn about how love worked if this was all they knew? As she read the report, her mind returned to Candy, and she felt the tight aching in her chest again. She would never get used to it. And though it hurt to carry so much trauma, she claimed that the day it stopped getting to her was the day she needed to quit.

Although this case would be perfect for Daniel, he had to prioritize the Ossie case, so she assigned it to another investigator in her unit.

The jangle of the phone interrupted her thought process. "Jennifer Riley," she spoke into the receiver.

"It's Michael."

"Hey. I meant to call you and catch up. You are still at the hospital?"

"Yeah," he answered. "I have been meeting with Chris and will fill you in on all I know as soon as possible. But first, I need a favor."

"Sure, what is it?"

"I finally got some contact information for the boy's family."

"How did you get that? Please tell me it was legal?"

She heard his chuckle. "It was. His pediatrician's practice is linked with the hospital, so the information was in his chart. We are the legal custodian now, as you always taught me, so I played that card and got the info."

"Good work," Jennifer said. "What did you find out?"

"I found Dad. Well, I found his cell number, at least."

Jennifer exclaimed with delight. "No, kidding? Did you call him?"

"I did. I found out he lived in Baldwin County. Near Gulf Shores. And apparently, he was already on his way to Mobile."

"What? How did he know about his son?"

"He got a call from Mobile Infirmary about his wife's admission. He told me that he is still listed as her emergency contact because they are not divorced. His wife's psychiatrist called him to get permission for treatment. Remember, she was catatonic when they brought her in."

"Where's he been all this time his son has been kept prisoner and tortured?" Jennifer hated that she was already judging him.

"Jennifer, that man sounded shaken up. I believe him when he says he had no idea this was happening."

"What do you mean?"

"He claims he had no idea how bad his wife had become. And certainly, didn't know she was mistreating Chris. The kid was always her favorite, according to him."

"Did he say why he moved to Baldwin County?"

"According to him, his job transferred there. We didn't talk much because he said he was almost in Mobile and wanted to come to the office immediately."

"And you want me to interview him?"

"Chris is starting to warm to me, and I want to spend more time with him to see if he will open up. So yes, if Dad gets there before I can get away, can you please talk with him?"

"Absolutely," said Jennifer. "I will tell Pat to buzz me when he comes in. Meanwhile, see if you can get the clearance for us to talk with Mom at the Infirmary. I haven't had a chance to get a request in. If you can clear it for tonight, I will go by this evening."

"You sure? I don't mind interviewing her myself. I should be through here in a couple of hours."

"I know you are up to the challenge, Michael. That's not it." She quickly added, "I think she might open up to a woman. Something tells me she is not very trusting of men right now."

"You might have a point," conceded Michael.

14

Chris

Michael spent much of the morning with Chris, gathering information about his family, his school, and his likes and dislikes. The child demonstrated a wary but affable affect. When Michael tried to broach the subject of Chris' brother, Billy, however, the young boy's eyes filled with tears. After a couple of incidents, Michael slipped out of the room to update Jennifer and to let her know about Mr. Barry. As he returned to the room, Michael saw that Chris was enjoying a bowl of applesauce.

"Every time I come in here, you are eating something. How do you get those nurses to keep bringing you food? What is your secret?"

Chris smiled, his face turning pink. "They just come in and bring me stuff."

Michael watched the boy take small bites of the pureed apples, smiling contently after each spoonful. Chris was probably not hungry, but since he had been deprived for so many months, he equated food with safety and security. Knowing the next few questions would be difficult, Michael took a slow breath in. He hated dragging that poor kid back down into the basement, but he had to try and get some answers.

"Chris, I know that I just keep asking questions. And you are probably so tired of me. Do you know why I am asking questions?" he asked.

Chris stopped chewing and looked at the social worker. His head cocked to the side, reminding the social worker of his lab Jester, all the while chewing as he processed. He finally answered. "To keep me safe?"

"Yes. That's right. Very good. To keep you safe. But what does that mean to you? What do you need to be safe from?"

"Keep me from being hit and locked in the basement again?"

"Chris," Michael looked compassionately at the child. "I promise you this: I will make sure that you never get locked in that basement again. I want you to know that you are safe now. No one can hurt you in here."

The boy nodded quietly.

"But you are right again. Very smart. You see, the more I know about how you came to be in the basement, the more I will be able to figure out how to help you find a place where you feel like you belong."

"I used to belong to my family." Chris' head bowed, and his eyes lowered. "Until Billy died. Guess I don't have a family anymore."

Michael mentally kicked himself at the poor word choice. "Well, one of the things I want to find out is where your family is now. We know your mother is at another hospital, but I want to learn about the other family. Your dad for one."

"He left me too," the boy stated flatly.

"I know, but I want to find out why. Maybe there's a reason we don't know yet. Maybe your family can be helped to take care of you without hurting you. It's like a big mystery. Do you like mysteries?"

"Billy used to read me the Hardy Boys books. They belonged to my dad when he was little. And Harry Potter. Those were kind of like mysteries, right?"

"In a way. Mysteries are just answers we haven't found yet. And I was hoping you could help me solve this mystery. Can you do that?"

Intrigued, Chris nodded.

"But here's the hard part," said Michael. "To do that, I might ask you some scary questions."

"About the basement?"

Michael saw a tremor in Chris' hand. "Yes, about the basement and even before that. But if you are still scared to talk about that, we can do it another day."

Chris' eyes flashed suddenly as he shouted, "Hey! I ain't scared!"

The outburst did not surprise Michael. He knew that the trauma Chris had been through created a confusing tangle of emotions and conflicts.

"Okay, Chris. I can see you are not scared. But if you were, it would be fine. You know what buddy? Even I get scared sometimes."

The boy retorted. "You are a big person. Adults don't get scared, do they?"

Michael smiled. "Sometimes everyone gets scared. So, can we talk about what happened in the basement?"

"Will it help us figure out why she did it?"

Michael knew. 'she' was Chris' mother. "It may help us to understand. Sometimes, though, people get sickness in their mind and do things they wouldn't have done without that sickness."

"Does my momma have a sickness in her mind?"

"Yes, son. She does." Patting his hand, Michael added. "And she is at the hospital getting help for that sickness right now."

Chris sat quietly for a few minutes, digesting the information, before he turned to Michael and said, "Okay. I can talk about it. I want to help you solve the mystery."

"Are you sure?" Michael asked.

Chris nodded solemnly.

"You want just to tell me like a story, or do you want me to ask questions?"

"I don't know. You start."

"Let's start with your brother. Tell me about Billy. Sounds like he was a really cool dude."

Chris' smile wavered, but he answered. "Billy was the best at everything. He was good at sports and school and even could play the guitar."

"I bet he had a lot of friends," encouraged Michael.

"Yeah. He did. But he loved me, even though I couldn't play baseball or do good in school like him."

"Did you want to play baseball?" Michael wondered.

"Not really, but I know some of his friends made fun of me because I was no good at sports. Billy would get really mad at them if they did. He always took up for me."

"Sounds like a good big brother to me."

"He was." Chris looked wistful. "I miss him a lot."

Michael patted the small hand. "I know you do. You are doing so good remembering.

The boy beamed.

Michael pressed forward. "Were you there when Billy got hurt?"

All he got was another nod.

"Chris, I can't even imagine how scary it was to see that. Do you want to talk about it?"

This time, the boy shook his head quickly, and Michael changed the questions. Chris would need intensive trauma work to process that day. Michael would ensure that the service was scheduled immediately.

"What did your mom and Dad do after Billy passed away?"

"Huh?" questioned the boy.

"After he died."

Chris's lips turned downward as he struggled not to cry. "Oh. Well, Mom went to the hospital, having one of her spells. She didn't even come to the funeral."

"What about your dad?"

Chris closed his eyes and took a breath. "He cried and cried. All the time. Billy was his favorite."

"You were left all alone. That must have been very lonely. What did you do?" probed the social worker.

"After the funeral, I just stayed in my room. I was mad and sad and scared all at the same time."

"Did anyone take care of you while your mom was in the hospital and your dad was so sad?"

"Well," admitted Chris, "Daddy tried. He did the cooking and even tried to make me come out and play with him some."

There was a moment of quiet before the child continued. "But Michael?"

"Yes? What is it?"

"I just didn't want to see him. And I didn't want him to see me. I thought if he saw me, he would feel sadder that I wasn't Billy and cry some more. So, I just stayed in my room."

"You didn't want to make him sadder."

"No," said Chris. But then momma came home from the hospital, and I was happy to see her. I thought I could go to her, and she would let me play by her in the big bed and make me feel better about Billy."

"And did you? Go to her?"

Michael noticed the tears forming in the corners of Chris' eyes. Maybe they should take a break, he thought. But even as he started to suggest it, the boy continued.

"I did. But she wouldn't talk to me. I tried to tell her I was sad, too. But she just acted like I was invisible. Even when she did talk to me, she kept calling me Billy." The tears began to spill over onto his cheeks. "I said, 'momma, it's not Billy, I'm Chris.' But she just kept asking me why I left her?"

Michael blanched, feeling the lump form in his throat. "That must have been so sad and scary for you."

"Then, daddy left too."

"Tell me how that happened.."

Chris' face twisted in pain, but he went on. "He came into my room one night and told me he was leaving. I said, 'Where are you going, daddy?' And he said he was moving to the beach because of his job. I asked him if Momma and I would be moving too. But he said no. He said that momma needed some time away from him because she was sad about Billy."

Michael squeezed the little boy's hand but didn't dare interrupt the flow.

"How could he leave us? I mean, Billy was dead; momma was still sick. Who was gonna take care of me?" After that outburst, it was as if he had deflated. Chris lay back on the bed, pressing his eyes closed as tears filled them.

"I'm so sorry that you had to go through that," Michael said quietly. "You are so brave to be able to tell me all of this. But you look really tired. You want to take a little break?"

Chris nodded silently. Then asked. "Can I have some coke?"

"Sure, I'll step out and get you one. When I come back, we will see how you feel about finishing up."

Chris smiled, his cheeks and eyes wet. "But I didn't tell you about the basement yet."

Michael turned. "No, you didn't. Not yet. But you are helping me unravel this mystery a little at a time. You are doing a great job! Let me get you that coke, and then you can tell me."

The walk to vending allowed Michael to process his own feelings. Listening to Chris Barry pour out much trauma that he had experienced in his young life had been extremely difficult. The events of his life seemed to be designed to break him down. But it was amazing how resilient the boy seemed. Not just physically but psychologically. Whatever toxin had been introduced to his body seemed to have flushed out, and the boy was getting stronger physically. And emotionally, for him to have experienced such trauma, Chris was showing an amazing ability to connect with others on an emotional level. What a survivor he was, mused Michael.

Returning to the room with an ice-cold drink, Michael saw that Karen had also returned to take vitals.

"Is he going to make it, nurse?" he joked.

Karen smiled down at the bed. "This young man is doing so good; I might give him a milkshake tonight!"

"Really?" squealed Chris. "With fries?"

"Milkshake and fries? What kind of cave boy are you?" she laughed.

"Billy used to dip his fries into ice cream, and it was so good!"

Gathering her clipboard, she turned to go. "We'll see. You never can tell."

Michael poured the cola into a cup of ice before handing it over. Billy drank long from the straw and hummed his appreciation.

"So are you okay for us to finish up? If you are tired, I can come back tomorrow."

"No, I want to get it all out today and then we will be done, and your mystery is solved, and you can keep me safe."

Michael marveled at how the young boy's mind processes worked.

"Here we go. If you want to stop at any time, just say stop!" Understand?"

"Yeah."

"After your dad left, your momma put you in the basement." He watched carefully to see if the boy would shut down.

"Not at first. At first, she seemed okay after Dad left. I was surprised she didn't go into her blue time. But she didn't. She cleaned a lot, cooked a lot of food. and even started sewing again."

"Really? "Michael guessed that the manic episode of mom's bipolar disorder had kicked in.

"Yeah," confirmed Chris. "But she stopped talking to me. I mean, not even to say hi. And then, she would look really mean at me if I asked her something or got in her way. She stopped calling me Billy, but she didn't call me Chris either."

"What did she call you?

"She started calling me 'boy'."

"Boy? Just boy?"

Chris' shoulders slumped, and he laid back in the bed. "Just boy. Like I didn't even have a name."

"What did you do?"

"I tried to stay out of her way mostly. I ate cereal when I was hungry, or sometimes she would leave food on the table for me, and I would eat that and wash my plate really good."

Chris went on. "But I guess I wasn't very good at washing because she would always find spots on the plate, and she would yell at me."

"Did she hit you?"

Chris nodded. "She spanked me with a belt when I was bad, which was about every day. Then, one day, she got so mad she scratched my face like a cat!"

Michael had seen the old linear scars across his left cheek.

"I learned to just be really quiet. You know, so I wouldn't get in trouble."

Michael nodded.

"One day, she came into my room while I was asleep. I just got some brand-new Iron Man pajamas sent to me from my Uncle Rudy for my birthday. I had plum forgotten that it was my birthday," he said with a hollow laugh.

"Your birthday?" Michael repeated.

"I was nine years old! Almost a teenager!"

That brought a smile to the face of the social worker. "She came into your room," he prodded, knowing he was getting to the crux.

"Yeah. She made me get out of bed, and she took me down into the basement. She told me I was going to live down there now."

"Did she tell you why you had to live in the basement?"

"She told me that there were evil things in the world that wanted to kill me. They had told her so, and I had to hide from them down there."

"Wow. That must have been so scary."

Chris was obviously remembering the moment. His hands began shaking again.

"I cried and begged her not to leave me there in the dark. I promised her I would be good! Then she said that I was a child of the devil, but she was a good mother, so she still had to keep me safe."

Michael was startled. "Of the devil? What did she mean?"

Shrugging his thin shoulders, Chris said, "I don't know. She hardly talked to me after that. She would come down sometimes and bring me cheese sandwiches and water. Sometimes, she would forget. At first, I cried each time I saw her and begged her to let me come back up. But when I did, she got mad and hit me or sometimes would just not come down for a whole day or two."

"Chris," Michael said softly.

"I thought I was gonna die that last day. The day you guys found me. I wasn't even scared about it. I thought it would be nice to see Billy up in heaven."

"Did she give you something that day that made you sick?" Michael did not know if Chris knew he had been drugged.

"I dunno. She made me oatmeal. It tasted so good. But then my tummy hurt, and I threw it all up. I felt so sick. My head and my stomach hurt so bad! I started crying and yelling when it hurt. I guess making all that noise made momma mad, cuz next thing I knew, she had locked me in the freezer. And that's all I know until I got here."

Chris began slurping at his coke again, trying to smile, but his eyes were fearful.

Michael walked over to the bed and ruffled the small boy's hair. "Chris, you have survived like a superhero, you know that. I want you to know how proud I am that you could tell me that whole story. It was hard to talk about, I know. I think I have solved the mystery with your help."

Chris continued to drink. "Will it help you find a family to take care of me?"

"Well, I definitely think any family would be lucky to have you in their home. But what would you say if I told you I found your dad?"

Chris stopped drinking, pulling the straw from his lips?" Daddy? Is he here?"

"He is not here yet, he just found out what happened and wanted to drive all the way here to make sure you are okay. He wanted to come by and see you later tonight. But only if you want to see him."

"You mean he really wants to see me? He's not mad about me getting momma into trouble?"

"No, Chris. He is not mad at you at all. Your dad is very worried about you. He does want to see you to make sure you are safe and to tell you how sorry he is that he left."

"He is sorry?" asked Chris.

"I am going to let him tell you that. If you want to see him?"

Chris bobbed his head. "I do, Michael. I do."

15

Daniel

Daniel stood on the sun-tinted front stoop and knocked. On the door, which had been painted a rich mocha, hung a decorative burlap cross embellished with miniature needlepoint roses. Several seconds passed with no answer, so he knocked again. Voices were coming from inside the home, but he could not tell if it was a person or a television that had been left on. Sometimes, his elderly clients leave the TV on when they're gone to make it seem occupied. The reasoning behind the trick was sound. Typically, burglars seek out houses that are unoccupied to avoid unnecessary complications. Easy-in. Easy out.

He had hoped to talk with Miss Katz this morning and complete the collateral contacts needed for his investigation. Getting her input into the events leading up to Carrie's death could firm up the timeline he had been creating. As Jennifer alluded, sometimes neighbors know more than they initially let on. Miss Katz could hold the key to whoever hurt the baby. It was a long shot, but one he wanted to tackle.

Not today, Daniel. Miss Katz is either not home or does not want company.

The Katz home was identical in style to many on the block, yet it stood out from the others. Most structures in the older neighborhood desperately needed a face-lift, but this home appeared to have come directly from the plastic surgeon. Bright yellow siding complemented by pale brown window frames and the mocha door lifted the overall look of the home. Daniel wasn't crazy about what he considered the garishness of the yellow, but he had to admit that it was the best-looking home on the block.

This lady wanted to shine.

Her lawn also spoke of fastidiousness and care. Freshly mown, it was framed by neatly trimmed shrubs and a small circle of plastic pansies surrounding the mailbox.

In stark contrast stood the Ossie home to Daniel's left. While identical in framework and construction, the similarities ended there. The Ossie home had once been constructed of beige vinyl siding. Green and black streaks of grime, dirt, and mildew crawled up the front and sides like a contagion, slowly consuming the house from the outside.

Shingles on the sloping porch were dangling at the ledge, waiting for an opportune time to fall. The front lawn of the Ossie home had not seen a mower in months, now more of a meadow with long, flowing grass. Why had the city not intervened, he thought?

That yard is a haven for rodents or even snakes.

As Daniel observed the home where little Carrie lived and died, his gaze caught a dark blue color peeking behind the house. Descending the stairs from Miss Katz's house, he walked toward what he had assumed as an empty Ossie home. As he neared, he saw a 90's style blue Taurus parked in the backyard.

Someone's there. No way I'm that lucky.

Daniel decided to chance it and crossed the tall grass to the porch. As he rapped on the door, he noticed that one of the front windows sported cardboard sheets instead of glass.

He was struck by the fact that the state of the house mirrored the state of the family: broken and seemingly in ruin. He knocked again.

The door jerked open, and the man in the doorway glowered. "Who are you, and what the hell do you want?"

He appeared to be in his thirties, with a sallow pock-marked face. Brown hair had been cut military style, revealing red sores on his scalp. The man wore a grey cotton T-shirt over red gym shorts, both torn. Most remarkable were his arms, covered in numerous red whelps, like bee stings. The stench emanating from him made Daniel cough.

Clearing his throat, Daniel asked. "Are you Brian McArthur?"

"Who wants to know?"

Daniel displayed his badge and added, "Daniel Bradshaw. I am with the Mobile County Department of Human Resources. I wanted to talk with you about Carrie Ossie."

Unblinking and surly, the man asked, "What do you want to talk to me for? Weren't my kid. I don't know nuthin'."

Daniel continued. "I just need to ask you a few questions. BJ said that you were here with her when Carrie stopped breathing. Is that right?"

"Bitch implicates me?"

Daniel added quickly, "She has not implicated you in anything. I need to figure out what happened."

"Sounds like you think I did something."

"I'm not implying anything." Daniel's patience was waning. "I just need to talk to everyone who was with Carrie. To get their side of the story, so to speak."

When the man grinned, Daniel grimaced at the stages of rot in his teeth.

"So I'm like some kind of witness?"

At first, Daniel is puzzled by the man's lack of concern or anxiety. But then he figured it out: Brian was high.

"Listen, Mr. Welfare Man," Brian continued. "I was just at the house to crash that night. BJ and Jason came to my crib, and she did some meth. BJ was tripping, so I went home with her. To, you know, take care of her."

"So BJ used, but you didn't?"

Brian cackled. "Hell. You got me there! Damn straight I got high. To be honest, I couldn't walk straight, let alone drive. BJ did get high with me, but I was the one tripping. She brought me here, and I crashed."

"Do you remember seeing Carrie that night?"

"Aren't you listening to me? I was out. O-U-T, out. I didn't see anybody. I barely remember the night at all."

Daniel lowered his voice to lessen the irritation that had to be leaking out. "Well, if you could tell me anything you do remember, it would be very helpful."

"Like I said. I was high, and I came here to crash. The last thing I remember is that BJ was going to get Carrie from that judgy preacher lady who watches her. I passed out before she got back. The next thing I know, BJ is screaming like a banshee."

"Judgy neighbor? You mean Miss. Katz?"

"Yeah, that bitch who lives next door was always preaching at BJ. Said if she didn't change her ways, God was gonna punish her."

"Punish her how?"

"How should I know? I don't get into all that religious goody-goody stuff. All's I know is BJ would get upset every time she went over there."

"So why did BJ keep using her?"

"I told her to stop taking the baby to that crazy old bat. But I guess a free babysitter is worth some grief." His grin, again, made Daniel look away.

"Did Miss Katz take care of Carrie often?" asked Daniel.

"I guess. Whenever BJ wanted to get away and let her hair down."

"And where is BJ now? Is she still at the police station?"

"No, they let her come home for now, but she left again to get us some grub. I can tell you this: She is scared they will come back and arrest her."

"Do you think she hurt Carrie?" Daniel wondered if Brian would be as protective of BJ as she was of him.

"Probably. She can get a little crazy! I wouldn't put it past her."

"But you didn't see her shake the baby?"

"Man, I done told you twice. I ain't telling you again. I was out."

"Right." Daniel barely kept the contempt out of his voice that time. "You were high. You crashed. BJ screamed."

"See, you ain't so stupid. Now you got it."

Daniel knew he had better leave then. He had learned long ago not to get into a battle of wills with an addict. He handed the man his business card. "Would you take my card and let me know if you hear from BJ? I just want to talk with her."

"Hell No!" Brian yelled. "I ain't no snitch." And with that, the door slammed, and the interview ended.

Daniel stood on the porch for a few minutes, digesting what he had seen and heard. He hadn't checked in with the police that afternoon and knew they had picked up Ms. Ossie for questioning earlier. He was seething at the uncaring, narcissistic Brian McArthur. But he worried about BJ's state of mind. Had she left town? For some reason, he doubted it because she really seemed to care for her son.

Once again, he was grateful that Jason, their other child, was in foster care. What kind of life had he been living while his mother spiraled downward and his father was free-falling even faster? He could tell by the meth sores, the poor hygiene, and the rotting teeth that Brian was using hardcore.

Daniel crossed through the weeds, praying he would not see a snake. His car, still parked in the driveway of Miss Katz's home, was joined by another, a red Corolla. Behind the wheel was an elderly African American woman. His face, pinched with annoyance and frustration, relaxed at the sight.

Now, I can kill two birds in one trip.

16

Jennifer

Jennifer entered the large, open lobby, noticing that the Halloween decorations that had adorned the walls for October had already been replaced with a Thanksgiving theme. The bulletin board to the right of the door was covered in at least fifty hand-print turkeys. From the size of their hands, she could tell the creators were children.

"Nice work," she whispered to the receptionist. "You didn't waste any time." For which she got a brief smile as the young worker handed an appointment card to a departing client.

It was noon, and the lobby was almost devoid of people. A small child, pushing a plastic dump truck with his hand, drove the toy between the legs of a woman, who was oblivious to the vroom-vroom noises he was making with each forward push. She thumbed quickly through the pages of a Parenting magazine with a bored look. Jennifer guessed by her demeanor she was either a relative or a case aide.

Her eyes skimmed the rest of the room until she found him. Mr. Barry wore khaki slacks, a green polo shirt with a navy belt and navy shoes. He was clean-cut and shaven, appearing to be in his late 40s. His hands clasped and unclasped repeatedly, yet his eyes focused on the entrance. Jennifer strode toward the man and noticed the wariness in his eyes.

"Mr. Barry?"

He stood as if summoned. "Umm. Yes?"

Jennifer offered her hand. "I am Jennifer Riley, a CPS supervisor. Michael got hung up, so I am here to talk to you about your son."

He took the proffered hand in a firm handshake. "Yes, where can we go to talk?"

"There's a private interview room across the hall. We can go there."

Jennifer led Mr. Barry to the interview room, which was furthest from the lobby center. The room held a desk and two chairs but was otherwise empty. She crossed the room and took the chair behind the desk, knees resting on the red panic button affixed under the interview desk. After a close call in which a mentally ill client had tried to choke their worker, the panic button was installed. Pressing the red button alerted both the front and security desk, eliciting an immediate response. However, during all her time at DHR, Jennifer never had to use the panic button, but she appreciated its need.

Mr. Barry entered the office and sat in the chair facing the desk. "Where is Chris?" he asked.

Jennifer cleared her throat and began. "Mr. Barry, I understand you have questions and want some answers. I do, too, so let's review everything together to find those answers.

"What do you need to know?"

"I heard you were told about what has been happening with Chris."

His voice was slow and tinged with sadness. "I could not believe it when the hospital called me. I never thought she would do something like this. Chris was her pet." he sputtered.

Jennifer interjected. "It's okay, Mr. Barry. As I said, we are both here to find out what happened. But to do so, I will have to ask you some rather hard questions."

He nodded wordlessly.

"As you know, Chris is currently in our custody due to being unsafe with his mother. You just mentioned that you have been apprised of what has happened. What can you tell me?"

Mr. Barry crossed his arms and took in a deep breath. "I got a call from Mobile Infirmary early this morning."

"About your wife?"

"Yes. I am still listed as her emergency contact. The doctor discussed her psychiatric condition."

"Which is? We haven't talked to her doctor yet," admitted Jennifer.

"Oh. Well, she has had a history of ups and downs, but this time, the doctor said she had schizoaffective disorder with an acute psychotic break. When she first came in, she couldn't move or speak."

"Has that changed?"

"The doctor said she is beginning to come out of the catatonia."

"Okay. Will you give me permission to see and interview her at some point later? I want to hear what she has to say as well."

"You and me both," he nodded. Yes, I will add your name to the list."

"Sorry to digress, Mr. Barry. "What did the doctor tell you about Chris?"

"I was told Chris had been abused and neglected by Martha to the point he was hospitalized. They didn't have all the details because, as I said, Martha was non-verbal when she first came in. As soon as I heard, I got in the car and drove up from the Gulf to find answers. That's when that DHR worker called me."

"That was Michael. He is the one assigned to Chris' case."

"Yes. Michael, I remember. But when I asked him to tell me what happened to Chris and when I could pick up my son, he told me to come here."

His voice began to shake. "That's why I am here. No one will tell me about my son. I want answers. I want to see my boy!"

Jennifer spoke softly and calmly to de-escalate the man. "Mr. Barry. I promise you that you will see Chris today. But you are going to have to calm down. We need to get all the information on what happened to decide on the best way to keep Chris safe."

Wiping his eyes with the back of his hand, the man nodded silently.

Jennifer continued. "Mrs. Barry was admitted to the psychiatric floor of Mobile Infirmary last night, but it wasn't her first time to be admitted there. I understand that she has battled depression for some time."

A slight frown crossed his face, and he shook his head. "Martha had her highs and lows. But for a very long time, she had everything under control. She took her pills, and they worked. We were happy."

Jennifer let the silence linger.

His voice faltered. "Until we lost Billy."

"I'm sorry." she offered and watched as his eyes closed–tears pooling in the corner of his eyes. "She became more depressed. Did she stop taking her pills?"

He nodded. "More like she went into a hole, and well, she just never came back."

"Tell me about that," prodded Jennifer.

"Tell you about Billy, or the downward spiral of Martha, or why I left?"

"Yes."

Mr. Barry sighed and shifted again. "You know that my oldest son Billy was killed almost three months ago."

"Yes. Again, I am deeply sorry for your loss. I cannot even imagine the pain your family endured."

"Struck by lightning. Darndest thing, I mean, what are the odds?" Mr. Barry looked down, seemingly lost in a memory.

"Your whole family was devastated." Jennifer urged him to continue.

"Yes. We all took it hard—Martha and I… and Chris. Billy was smart, funny, and athletic. In baseball, he was a damn protégé. So yeah, it was tough. Martha had to be hospitalized for a spell."

"How long?"

"I don't remember exactly, about two weeks, it seemed like. They changed her meds, which seemed to help a little. But she never seemed to get that spark back. It was like she was not really there anymore."

"That must have been very difficult for you and Chris."

He nodded, looking at his shoes. "Chris." The threatening tears trickled down his cheek as a small sob escaped his lips. He took in a slow, deep breath before continuing. "My poor little boy. I was so caught up in my own grief I forgot to hold on to him. He lost his brother and his mother at the same time."

Jennifer listened. "What do you mean he lost his mother?"

"She just started to ignore him, acting like he wasn't even there. I became the mother and the father then. I ensured he went to school, ate supper, and had clean clothes."

"How did your son react to the change?"

Mr. Barry uttered a short, mirthless laugh. "People always thought that Chris was autistic or slow. But really, he was smarter in some ways than Billy, especially about people. Chris instinctively seemed to know that he needed to be invisible. He went to school, he bathed, he slept, he ate, but he also seemed to draw into himself."

"Did you try to reach out to him?" Jennifer tried to stifle the judgment in her voice.

His voice tinged with indignation. "Of course, I tried to reach him! Despite what this looks like, I love my son."

"I believe you, Mr. Barry; I must ask these questions."

Mr. Barry's voice seemed to lower. "I tried to talk to him at the house when I came home from work. I tried to get him to get up and do things, like go to the movies with me, play catch outside, or just do anything. But the truth of the matter is, he was his mother's boy. Her emotional abandonment of him seemed to take away everything but his basic instincts."

"That is incredibly sad. He missed his brother and the way his family used to be."

Covering his face with his palms, Mr. Barry cried, no longer trying to stench the flow.

Jennifer plucked a tissue from the box on the desk and handed it to him, allowing him the space to grieve. He took the Kleenex she offered him, dabbed his eyes, and blew his nose loudly.

After several minutes, he lifted his head again. Despite the redness of his eyes, his jaw was set. "No matter what you may think, I loved both my boys. But it seemed that I lost them both at the same time."

"I believe you. Tell me more about Chris."

"I told you that people thought Chris was autistic. Martha never believed that. But we had him tested anyway, and he wasn't autistic; he was just different. The psychologist told us that we should let him develop the interests that met his personality and not try to turn him into Billy's clone."

Jennifer smiled. "That was very good advice."

Mr. Barry smiled, "It turned out Chris was more mechanical. He could take apart a toaster and figure out how it went back together, and Billy wouldn't even begin to know how to do that."

"When did you last see or speak to Chris?"

Looking down, the man mumbled something she could not understand.

"I'm sorry, I didn't understand you."

He blurted out, "It's been five weeks. Five weeks. I know what you're thinking. How could I let it go on that long? I know I am a terrible father. I loved my son, yet I let Martha drive me away."

After a few seconds, Jennifer, ignoring the outburst, asked, "Tell me what happened that caused you to leave."

"I was in hell. My wife was a zombie who needed constant prodding to even get out of bed, and my own kid would rather play on a computer than acknowledge my existence. As Martha finally came out of the depression (or so I thought) and was able to manage the household, I started to hope again. I begged her to go to counseling with me so we could work out how to keep our family together. I loved her and Chris and just wanted to be happy again."

"Did she agree?"

His breath sounded ragged. "No."

Jennifer remained silent. She knew there was more.

Mr. Barry then said quietly. "She told me I killed Billy." His lips became a thin line. "She said that I was the one who wanted Billy to play baseball. I was the one who told us we couldn't miss the last game and that the rain would hold off. She said I killed Billy just as if I had struck him down myself. And that she would never forgive me."

"I am so sorry, Mr. Barry. That must have been very painful to hear."

"She told me to leave her and Chris alone! I couldn't believe it! I tried to tell her she wasn't thinking right, but she kept screaming for me to get out. So I did."

"Where did you go?"

"My job had an opening in the Gulf Shores office. The position was a promotion, and I had been trying to talk to Martha about it for over a year. When she kicked me out, I figured I would take it and get a house ready there until Martha could come to her senses and move down there."

"Did you try to keep in touch with them?"

"Of course, I tried. I called Martha and Chris daily for the first two weeks, but no one answered. I left messages. I said I loved them. I said I wanted to see my son. But no one ever called me back."

He ran a hand across his forehead. "After a while, I just stopped trying. And now, to find out my son has been abused while I was only an hour away? How do you think I feel?"

Jennifer leaned toward him, her hands clasped in front of her. "Mr. Barry, I imagine you feel devastated. I can hear it in your voice. And I believe you. We need to clear up a few more things so we can plan for you to see Chris."

He held up a finger. "I will do whatever you ask of me. But I need you to hear that If I had known for one second that she was mistreating Chris, I would have called the sheriff and would have gone to my house and taken my son out of harm's way. I didn't know." He wiped his eyes again and muttered. "I just didn't know."

17

D aniel

Much like her home, Ida Mae Katz stood out among her neighbors. Daniel guessed she was in her seventies, but he couldn't be sure. She wore a blue paisley jacket over tan slacks with a lighter blue blouse peeking under the coat. Her white hair had been cut into a stylish wedge, and her make-up looked like a professional had applied it.

He stopped on the sidewalk so as not to frighten her and waited for her to notice him.

She, however, seemed preoccupied with something in her purse. *She can't find her keys.*

When he cleared his throat, she quickly glanced in his direction, first fear, then suspicions clouding her features.

"Miss Katz?" Daniel began.

"Yes, I am. And who are you?"

"My name is Daniel, and I am with the Department of Human Resources. May I show you my badge?"

She sized him up warily. "Yes. But stay the way you are. Show me from there."

He held up the laminated badge with his picture and the agency name on it. He knew she couldn't see it from that distance but wouldn't have admitted it.

"So, you are who you say you are. Now, what do you want with me?"

"Daniel approached her slowly. "I am investigating the Ossie family. I would like to ask you a few questions if you have just a few minutes."

"Investigating them for what?" she had not let her guard down. "Did she get arrested? Did something happen to the kids?"

"Would you be surprised if I said yes?" he asked her.

"No. They live the devil's lifestyle over there. But, Mr. Bradshaw, you have not answered my question. What are you investigating?"

"I am investigating the death of BJ's daughter."

The color seemed to drain from her face. "Carrie's dead?"

Daniel could have kicked himself for such a rookie mistake. He had just assumed the whole neighborhood knew about the child's death. "I'm sorry that you had to find out this way. Please forgive me for just blurting that out. But, yes, Carrie passed away early this morning."

"Little Carrie's dead?" Her hand went to her throat, and she gasped like she was going to pass out. Her face flushed bright red; he noticed her breathing became faster.

Daniel rushed to the older woman's side and took her arm. She did not protest. He led her to the stoop of her home, where she sat on the top step, her hand on her chest.

"Are you okay?" he softly asked.

She waived away his question. "What happened to the child?"

"Are you sure that you are okay? You look pretty shaken up."

She gave Daniel a wilting glare. "Young man, you listen to me. I am 78 years old. And in those years, I have seen more tragedy than you have thought about. So yes, I am shaken, but don't mistake me for a feeble old fool. And don't coddle me. Just tell me how she died."

Daniel stifled the smile that threatened his face. She was definitely not feeble; at least, her tongue was not. "Carrie died from traumatic brain injury." He explained, "Someone shook her, and it caused her brain to swell."

Daniel thought he saw a glimpse of fear cross her eyes, but she quickly recovered. "How utterly tragic," she said as she shook her head. Listen, if you will give me a hand, we can go into the house. It is more comfortable than this old stoop."

She added, "I don't know what I can tell you, but I will help you any way I can."

Daniel proffered his arm again, and she took it. Rising to her feet, she led the way into the sun-yellow house with Daniel following her.

The home's interior, as immaculate as the exterior, contained antiques, collectibles, and comfortable furnishings. Miss. Katz apparently loved needlepoint, as evidenced by the multiple framed pieces throughout her home. Daniel noticed that each piece espoused religious references. In the hallway, he read "Idle Hands are the Devil's Handiwork," which had been mounted next to another one that said, "Vengeance is Mine Sayeth the Lord." As they passed through the living room toward the dining area, he noticed a large needlepoint over the mantle that read, "God is always watching you."

Daniel felt a little uncomfortable and, frankly, could see why Brian called her "judgy." But while it certainly was not his cup of tea, he would not draw any inferences from the decorations.

Miss Katz led him to a wooden dining table, which was set with floral china and linen napkins resting in gold rings.

"I'm sorry," said Daniel. "Are you expecting company? I can come back if this is a bad time."

At first, she looked confused, and then her eyes fell on the dressed tabletop, and she laughed. "No, my dear. I am expecting no one. But who knows what the day may bring? My mother taught me to always have the table set because you never know when God will send someone your way."

Nodding, Daniel glanced up at the framed Needlepoint that had been hung over the doorway leading into the kitchen. It proclaimed, "If you don't work, you don't eat." He wondered if that was from the Bible as well.

"Miss Katz, maybe God did send someone to you today, and that person may be me." He smiled.

"Perhaps," she smiled. "Perhaps."

"Your house is charming," Daniel offered. "Is all the needlework yours?"

"It is. My mother also told me to keep my hands busy doing something useful, or they would be used for something evil."

"I can only imagine," he said. Although, really, he couldn't. "Do you live here alone?"

"Yes, I have always lived here alone."

"What about your husband?"

"I never married." She smiled coyly.

"Forgive my assumption. I thought Ms. Ossie told me you were a widow. I apologize, Miss Katz."

"It's okay. People see an old woman living alone and assume she's a widow. I had a beau once, but he fell out of Grace with God. I couldn't marry him after that."

Daniel didn't know what to do with that remark, so he changed the subject. "You cared for Carrie the night before she died, right?"

Again, he saw a veiled look pass over her eyes, but she answered plainly, "Yes. But she was alive when her mother picked her up."

"Oh, yes, Ms. Ossie confirmed that. I am just trying to establish a timeline."

Her face seemed to relax, and he went on. "Tell me as much as you can remember about that day."

She closed her eyes as if to arrange everything in her head. "BJ brought little Carrie over that afternoon. She asked me to watch her while she and Jason went to a cookout at some friends' home. At least, that is what she said. I figured she was going to go shoot up with that drug addict Brian."

Her voice had turned steely, Daniel noticed. But he did not say anything, and she continued.

"She didn't come to pick up Carrie until late at night. I was getting ready for bed when she called."

"About what time was that?" Daniel wondered if she would corroborate BJ's statement. "Eh, sometime between 10:30 and 11:00, I would say."

"And you were still up, right?"

"Yes. I stay up late because I don't sleep very well anymore, and it's no use tossing and turning. I used to say, I'll sleep when I'm dead." She laughed at her own joke.

Daniel interjected. "Tell me how Carrie seemed that night."

"She was a good baby as always. She was a little colicky around 7:00 pm, but I just rocked her and fed her a little cereal, and she quieted right down. So I laid her on the bed in the spare room surrounded by pillows."

"And she was still asleep when BJ picked her up?"

"Sound as a log," she confirmed.

"Was the colic a new thing?" asked Daniel, trying to understand what normal was for the infant.

"She normally did not fuss much, if that is what you mean," answered the old woman. "Carrie was a good baby, a sweet baby, considering she was born out of wedlock."

Miss Katz whispered conspiratorially, "All of BJ's babies were born out of wedlock. God will only put up with sin for so long, you know."

"What do you mean?" Daniel gently prodded.

"I mean that whole lifestyle: using drugs and having babies with different men makes God very unhappy. He only gives us so much latitude. And if we keep sinning, then he punishes us."

"Punishes us?"

She nodded vigorously, "God only punishes us because he loves us."

"And you think God punished Carrie by killing her?"

"Oh, my lord, no." she looked annoyed. "That's crazy. Please don't twist my words. Carrie was an innocent."

"I'm sorry," Daniel apologized again. "I didn't mean to upset you; just trying to understand what you are telling me. So God did not punish Carrie because her mother was a sinner?"

"Of course not." Her lips almost disappeared as she sucked them in. "He punished BJ by taking Carrie away from that life. Don't you see that Carrie's life, in that house of ungodliness, would have been as chaotic as that wild boy Jason's was? Carrie is in a much better place now and at peace with God."

Daniel, feeling uneasy with the tenor of the conversation, changed the line of questions. "So let me get this straight. BJ picked up Carrie between 10:30 and 11:00, and Carrie was asleep at the time."

"Hmmm, it was really closer to 11. I had just finished watching one of the late shows. Can't remember which one. But, as I said, I was about to go to bed."

"But Carrie was still asleep."

Her eyes flashed. "I said that already, didn't I?"

Daniel smiled. "Yes, ma'am. One more question. Have you ever seen Ms. Ossie or anyone else shake Carrie or harm her in any way?"

"No," she quickly responded. "Never seen anyone shake her or hit her. But they harmed her every time they put those drugs in their arms."

"Miss Katz," Daniel looked into her eyes. "It sounds like you really disapproved of their lifestyle, especially when it came to the welfare of the children. Can I ask you this? If you thought they were using drugs and the kids were being affected, why didn't you call the police or DHR?"

She sniffed. "Not my business to get in their lives. God's business."

Closing his notebook, Daniel stood to go. "Thank you so much for your time, Miss Katz. I won't keep you any longer. If I have any other questions, may I call you again?"

She smiled sweetly, the anger gone from her face. "Of course. I am always happy to help."

As Daniel opened the front door to leave, another framed needle-point perched on an easel caught his eye. It read, "Suffer the Little Children to Come unto Me."

He called Jennifer on his way back to the office.

"Hi, Daniel," she answered somewhat breathlessly.

"Did I catch you at a bad time?"

"No, the elevator was out at Mobile Infirmary, and I have to hike up a few flights of stairs."

"Mobile Infirmary? What are you doing there?"

"You have been so busy with the Ossie case that I haven't filled you in on what's going on with Michael's case. But in a nutshell, a mentally ill mother locked her 9-year-old in a basement for several months with limited food and water. It's possible she also gave him drugs or some sort of toxin, which caused him to be extremely ill."

Daniel whistled. "Is it a full moon week or what?"

He heard her laugh. "Sure feels like it. Michael is with the boy, and I arranged an appointment with the mother's therapist and the mother this afternoon. I'm headed up there now."

"You sound really busy. I'll update you later."

"No. I am about 30 minutes early. But let me get upstairs and stop heavy breathing in your ear, and I will call you back."

Daniel bit back the flirty retort that rose to his lips. Instead, he said, "I'll be here."

Ten minutes later, Jennifer called back. Daniel filled her in on the interviews with Brian McArthur.

"He sounds like a real dreamboat," she remarked. "It seems so unfair that he gets to walk away from all this because we can't prove anything."

"Well." Daniel tried not to sound as pleased with himself as he felt. "Maybe not free. I called up our buddy Detective Green and let it slip that I saw drug paraphernalia in the house. I bet Brian will be spending some time behind bars."

"Daniel? Did you see drug paraphernalia?"

"I saw rotten teeth and meth sores; he had to have something around there."

She sighed. "It's not that I don't agree that he needs to face consequences, but there are some things you should not tell your supervisor."

"What if I change the subject and tell you how creepy Miss Katz was?"

"Smart move," she agreed. "Creepy, how?"

"Something just wasn't right. Call it my gut. But she is definitely a little off. I'm coming back to the office later; I will give you the details. I'd love to get your take on it as well."

"Daniel? Do you think she hurt the baby?"

"Normally, she would be at the top of my list, but Carrie was fine when BJ picked her up. And I don't see that old lady hopping into a window at night to shake a baby."

Jennifer said, "I have to get off for now. I'm about to go talk to the psychiatrist while he has an opening. I'll call you back after my interview to talk again."

"Sounds good."

Daniel decided that when he got to the office, he would try to reach out to BJ Ossie again. He didn't trust Brian to tell the truth. Maybe she was still at the precinct? Reaching out to the desk sergeant would answer the question for sure. He really wanted to talk with her again. The nagging feeling persisted, and he didn't like unanswered questions.

<h1 style="text-align:center">18</h1>

Jennifer

The group therapy room on the seventh floor of Mobile Infirmary–painted a pink so pale that it was felt rather than seen–seemed to whisper calmness. White pleather chairs formed a circle to invite unity and support to the patients as they shared their trauma. Jennifer scrutinized the current occupants: Martha Barry and the Asian male nurse who escorted her from the doctor's office into the therapy room.

*****

Dr. Britain, the psychiatrist, had spoken with Jennifer earlier after receiving permission from Mr. Barry, who, as her husband, still had residual rights of decision-making. The psychiatrist walked her through his patient's condition. When she first arrived, Ms. Barry exhibited akinetic catatonia, with a lack of verbal response and wooden-like movement. Due to her acute condition, she could offer no information nor answer any questions from the police or even from his own staff. Dr. Britain, who had been treating Mrs. Barry since the death of her child, began adjusting her medication to promote a more stable outcome.

"Dr. Britain?" Jennifer had asked, "What happened after Billy died? Was she like this?"

He shook his head. "No. Martha struggled with cyclothymic depression for years but was on a regimen of cognitive-behavioral therapy and mild anti-depressants, which seemed to be working."

"I thought she was bipolar?"

Smiling, the doctor explained, "Cyclothymia does mimic bipolar affective disorder in that there are ups and downs, bouts of depression followed by bouts of mania. However, the highs and the lows are much lesser than actual bipolar disorder."

Jennifer documented the diagnosis and explanation before proceeding. "But you had never seen this akinetic catatonia?"

He shook his head. "No. Never. The condition in which she presented this admission displayed more psychotic features."

"So before Billy's death, she suffered from Cyclothymia. That was controlled with therapy and medication. Got it. What happened after Billy's death?"

Dr. Britain scratched his chin, absently pulling at the hair of his grey goatee. "Billy's death was sudden, violent, and traumatic. Ms. Barry retreated into herself completely but did not demonstrate catatonia. Due to the severity of the depression, I thought it best to have her admitted for a couple of weeks so that we could try and adjust her meds. We found a promising outcome with Celexa and Depakote. When she was discharged, she functioned better, and her moods were more stable."

Jennifer pushed. "Help me to understand how she went from stable to dangerous."

"Psychopharmacology is a tricky thing," he explained. "It could have been a reaction to the new meds, or the underlying condition could have been there all along. We won't know until we get more information, both physical and psychological."

"Has she said anything today?"

"Yes. Her catatonia has been resolved. However, the psychosis remains. Ms. Barry presents with a religious fixation that God speaks with her audibly, directing her actions. In other words, God told her to hide Chris in the basement. God told her to protect him from Satan, who had stolen Billy from her."

"Good Lord," Jennifer did not mean to utter the pun.

But it wasn't wasted on the doctor, who smiled. "Exactly."

Jennifer read over her notes before rising. "Dr. Britain, thank you so much for this; it's extremely helpful in understanding Ms. Barry's state of mind."

"Of course," he answered.

"One more thing, "she added. "Before I meet with her, is there something I should watch for? Be aware of?"

Dr. Britain thought before answering. "We've now added an anti-psychotic to her regimen, so I don't think you will get much from her. I have a nurse who will be sitting in the room with you at all times to ensure safety."

"For me or her?"

He smiled again, "For both of you."

Jennifer started toward the door leading into the group room. "Oh, I know I said it already, but only one more question. What is her prognosis?"

He shrugged. "She will always have a mental illness. All we can do is treat it with pharmacology and therapy. Will she be able to go home? Most certainly. If I am called on to testify in her child abuse trial, I will say that she should not be held accountable for her actions at the time due to her mental illness. But should she be allowed to parent Chris without supervision? The answer is no."

*****

In the therapy room, Ms. Barry stood with her back to the entrance, facing a large plate glass window. The nurse saw the concern in Jennifer's eyes and assured her that the window, double-paned with shatterproof glass, brought light and warmth to the room.

Jennifer appraised the woman who had yet to turn around and face her. Tall and very thin, Ms. Barry had a runway model's body. Her raven hair, with a few feathers of gray, had been swept back into a loose ponytail that floated to the middle of her back. She wore faded skinny jeans, a silk blouse, and a red cardigan. She seemed completely put together.

Jennifer whispered to the nurse. "I expected her to be in a hospital gown."

He leaned in and replied, "Dr. Britain lets them wear their own clothes as part of the normalcy process." He then turned back to Mrs. Barry.

"Martha," called the nurse. "There's a lady from DHR here to talk to you. Dr. Britain said you should go ahead and talk with her. She wants to talk about Chris."

Jennifer watched as Ms. Barry's body became rigid for a few seconds and then visibly relaxed. Whether it was by sheer force of will, she could not determine. Slowly, as the patient turned to face her, Jennifer could see that she had once been stunningly beautiful, with amber eyes that burned with an intensity that radiated off her in waves.

"Good afternoon," the woman said, her voice deep and clearly articulated with no trace of a Southern accent.

"Hello, Ms. Barry. My name is Jennifer."

As the nurse retreated to the corner of the room to jab at his cell phone, Ms. Barry said, "I guess I am really getting better if they let me have visitors."

"Do you feel you are getting better, Ms. Barry?" asked Jennifer.

The woman rolled her eyes. "Just call me Martha. It's much more honest." Her brow creased, "Do I think I am getting better?" she repeated the question. "Well, let's just say I don't feel worse. But wait, that's the incorrect answer, isn't it?"

"What do you mean?" questioned Jennifer.

"What do I mean? Silly girl. I mean, that I should feel worse, right? I mean, they tell me I tried to kill Christopher. So if I am getting better, I should feel really bad about that, shouldn't I?"

"And do you?" Jennifer knew better than to let herself be baited.

The deep-throated laugh sent a shiver through Jennifer. "How can I feel bad about something I don't even remember doing? Scenes run through my mind like in one of those Tarantino movies. But did any of it really happen? I don't remember."

"So you don't remember anything about the last three to four months?" Jennifer could sense the manipulation in the woman's measured words.

"No," Martha said calmly. "Not a thing. Therefore, you probably came all the way here for nothing. I understand if you want to leave now."

Jennifer leveled her gaze at the woman and said, "Ma'am, let's be very clear. I can't imagine what you have been through over the past several months. But I will have to assess whether, at some point, Chris can live with you again. To do this, I need to know what happened after your husband left and how the situation got so bad."

Mrs. Barry just looked at Jennifer, a cold glint in her eye.

Jennifer continued. "I'm finding it difficult to believe that you remember nothing. Especially since your doctor has already told me things that you do remember."

Martha's eyes narrowed. Her tone became decidedly colder. "Did he now?"

"He did. Now, let's start over. Can you please tell me what you do remember?"

Martha studied the social worker for several minutes before speaking. Jennifer kept up her gaze, never wavering until the woman spoke. "You may be operating under a false assumption, dear."

"Tell me."

"You assume I want Christopher back. Why on earth would I want him back? He is the reason I am in this hospital."

"Is he?" Jennifer clamped her teeth together.

"Had he not started that infernal screaming, no one would have come into my house; he would still be safe in the basement. And I would be at home making pumpkin bread. So yes, this is on him. I can no longer protect him."

Jennifer scrutinized the amber eyes. "Protect him? Were you told why he was screaming? You poisoned him, causing him to have severe abdominal pain. That is why he was screaming."

For the first time, her eyes looked puzzled. "Poison? Why would I poison him? How would I poison him? I gave him a few of my Celexa. They make me sleepy, so I thought they would make him sleep through Halloween."

Jennifer wrote in her notebook that she would share the information with Dr. Britain and the hospital. "So you were not trying to kill him?"

"Kill him?" her eyes narrowed. "My dear, I was trying to save him."

Understanding beginning to come to her, and though she knew the answer, Jennifer asked, "What were you saving him from?"

"Satan wanted to take him from me. God told me to hide him. But now, Satan will find him. Especially now that he is out in the open."

"Like Satan took Billy?"

"Yes, exactly like that."

"And do you know why Satan took Billy and wants to take Chris?" explored Jennifer.

Martha's face relaxed. "Of course I do. Satan wants my children because I loved my family more than I loved God."

"And that made Satan mad," Jennifer was confused.

"You really are simple, girl," said Martha.

"Enlighten me, "

"Satan wants everyone. I am not special; neither is my family. Satan even wants you. But God protects us. The Bible says to put nothing before God. But I tested him. I stopped going to church when we got busy. We had baseball, picnics, and family time. God is a jealous God. He removed his protection, and Satan went to work taking things from me, starting with Billy, then my husband. Christopher was all I had left. So I had to hide him."

Jennifer nodded. "So you kept Chris in the basement. You hid him from everybody, including God?"

Martha's eyes flickered briefly. "Yes, that is why I did it."

"Then help me understand, why did you stop feeding him, hit him, and make him scared of you?"

The flicker became steel. "Christopher would not submit. He kept testing me. Always crying and begging to go out, play outside, and come upstairs with me. He never understood my reasons, so he had to be punished so he would fall in line."

"You punished him to protect him. Is that what you are saying?"

"Yes, I was protecting him."

"But you were hurting him." Jennifer knew she was on thin ice and could alienate Ms. Barry. But she knew that she was not getting the whole story.

The smile that had been flaccid on the woman's face became as hard and cold as her eyes. "Fine. I believed Satan wanted Christopher, and I did try to protect him. But all that went to waste. Now I discovered that my 'innocent boy' was a spy."

"A spy?"

"For God."

Jennifer was confused. She knew that the woman had delusions, but the delusions were not even in accord with each other. "Martha, when did you discover Chris was a spy?"

"I didn't work it out until I saw Ken this morning."

"Your husband."

"Yes. Ken has always been there for me. No matter our problems, he would move heaven and earth to make sure we made it together. He loved me so much. But he looked at me this morning like I was a monster. That's when I put it together."

"Martha, what are you talking about?"

"Christopher is a spy for God. Satan didn't take Billy. I thought he had. That's why I tried to protect Christopher. But it wasn't Satan who killed my oldest son. Christopher killed him. Think about it."

Jennifer sighed. "Walk me through it, Martha. Why do you think Chris is responsible for any of this?"

"First of all, "She said quickly, her speech pressured. "Christopher was at the game when God took Billy. Christopher was always jealous of his big brother. He must have told God to kill him. Then he got into Ken's head, making him leave me alone. And finally, after all my protection and love, the first chance he got, he brought strangers into my home to lock me up. Now, do you see what I should have done?"

Jennifer wanted to hear her say the awful word, so she prodded. "What should you have done?"

"It's absurdly simple. I should have killed him when I had the chance."

Jennifer heard the eerie laughter coming from Martha's lips, but she remained silent.

The social worker rose. "Thank you, Martha. I appreciate you allowing me to speak with you and to hear your story. I have all I need for now."

Martha looked surprised. "That's it? I can go home?"

Jennifer shook her head and looked at her with compassion. "No, Martha, you need to stay here until Dr.. Britain says you can go home. I hope he can help you to get to that point."

"Bitch!" cried Martha. "You are part of it, too, aren't you?"

The nurse looked up suddenly at the outburst and quickly approached Jennifer.

"Everything okay?" he asked.

Jennifer smiled and nodded. "Yes, I am done here." She felt Martha's icy hatred on her back as she turned to leave.

*****

On her drive back to the office, Jennifer called Michael and told him about her interview with Chris's mother.

"I think it is going to be a while before she gets out," she concluded.

Michael told her about the conversation with Chris and that Chris wanted to see his father.

"You talked to him, Jennifer. What do you think? "

"You know, Michael. I think a tragedy happened in this family, and they all suffered. But as far as intentional abuse or neglect, I don't think Mr. Barry was involved at all."

She heard him sigh. "I am so glad to hear that. I'll arrange a visit between them this afternoon and observe them together."

"Sounds good," she agreed. "Hey, Michael, check with Chris' doctor. I know that they are looking for what she gave him that made him so sick."

"Yeah? Do you know what it is?"

"Mrs. Barry said she put some of her Celexa into his oatmeal. I googled it and found that Celexa can cause severe headaches, nausea, and vomiting. See if the doctor can confirm that."

"I will let you know this evening."

"Oh, and Michael?"

"Yes, ma'am?"

"After the visit, go home. You have spent all day up there. Don't come back in today."

"But my notes? I have to enter them," he protested.

"It will be at least five or six when you leave USA. You can enter your notes tomorrow morning before emergencies get divided out."

"You sure?"

"Yes, Go home. Take care of yourself. It is so easy to burn out here. Take the moments when you can."

"I did want to watch the Auburn special tonight. Coach is supposed to talk about the win last Saturday."

"Yes, well, don't get too used to the wins. You know you still have to play us after Thanksgiving, and we know what a massacre that will be," Jennifer chided.

"Michael goaded back, "Lord, protect me from a Bama fan."

The phone rang as soon as Jennifer pulled into her parking space at the office. It was the intake line; a new emergency must be coming their way. Taking a deep breath, she answered with a cheerfulness she didn't feel, "Jennifer Riley."

19

Jennifer

Jennifer remained in her car, jotting down notes from the phone call. She had guessed correctly. A 12-year-old girl presented at school today with what appeared to be ringworm. The child told her teacher, however, that her mom's boyfriend had burned her with his cigarettes.

Jennifer was used to the confusion between ringworm and cigarette burns. Both left a circular, inflamed mark. But with cigarette burns, there was an almost charred edge. From the description sent into the intake, she bet this little girl had the latter.

Jennifer called a unit member and sent them out to the school. She then called the school principal to alert her that DHR was on the way and advised them not to send the girl home on the bus until her worker arrived. When she finished with a very worried school official, she turned to unbuckle her seat belt to get out of the car. Suddenly, a loud noise caused her to scream.

She whirled to see Daniel standing outside of her car. Although he had simply knocked on the window, Jennifer had been so far into her thoughts that the sound startled her. She depressed the button that unrolled her window. "Dammit, Daniel. You scared the crap out of me."

He laughed, which irritated her at first. But as the anxiety passed and she relaxed, she smiled as well.

"I waited out here for 10 minutes while you were on the phone," he offered. "I didn't knock until you were free. Didn't mean to make you jump."

He grinned again, "Although the look on your face."

"Yeah, Yeah, Yeah, get over yourself. Why are you lurking outside my car anyway?"

"I am lurking because I thought you wanted a debrief on the Ossie case."

Jennifer said, "Meet me in my office. It's hotter than hell stuck inside this car." She rolled her window up and opened her door.

Daniel leaned against the car. "I don't know about you, but I haven't eaten yet. I know it's almost two, but I wanted to grab a late lunch."

"Sure. Yeah, go eat," she smiled. "Come to think of it, I haven't eaten either. What does this job do to us?"

"I can go to Foosackly's and grab some chicken. Want me to bring back some for you?"

Jennifer thought for a moment. "Comfort food. Yummy. Okay. Just grab me a Number One and a Diet Coke. I will pay you when you get back."

Daniel teased. "So, our first lunch date, huh?"

Jennifer rolled her eyes. "Some date: fried chicken fingers and work. Just hurry up. Now, with you talking Foosackly's, I am starving."

She headed for the CA/N hall when he left to check in with her other staff. A couple of workers had seen her and asked for guidance on their cases. Kim turned in another case for early review, and Jennifer thanked her before heading to her office at the end of the hall. She sat at the small conference table just as Daniel had arrived with the lunch. The smell of the fried goodness made her mouth water and biting into the juicy tenders felt like the most satisfying thing she had done all day.

Daniel opened his bag and withdrew a chicken finger. "How about we delay the case talk and take a few moments just to enjoy the meal?"

Jennifer nodded, her mouth busy savoring a crispy French fry.

Moments passed in an easy silence as they started in on their meal. Daniel grinned at Jennifer as she dipped fries into the honey mustard sauce she had ordered.

"Fries and honey mustard? I thought you ordered the sauce for your chicken."

"Good fried chicken doesn't need sauce," she instructed. "Honey mustard is great with French fries, though. Here, "she dipped a fry into the sauce and held it to his mouth,"

He chewed the combination thoughtfully before declaring. "Nope, don't see it. Ketchup is for fries and nothing else."

She laughed. "That decides it then. All your taste is in your mouth." She popped another mustard-dipped fry into her mouth to prove the point.

"Oh, now you are just being ridiculous. Do you eat ketchup on bananas?"

She chuckled. "Nope. But I do love a banana sandwich with mayonnaise."

"Ugh," he quipped. "That's enough. Now I can't eat anymore." He crumpled up the bag.

Jennifer picked up the bag and opened it. "Whatever. You ate everything in the bag. Don't pin that guilt on me!"

They laughed together. It was comfortable and intimate. When Jennifer realized what was happening, she shifted the conversation quickly: "Since you are through and I am not, go ahead and tell me about this babysitter while I eat."

"Back to work, boss?" his eyes were watching her.

Jennifer nodded and continued eating.

Daniel seemed slightly disappointed but then began recounting his visit with Miss Katz. Jennifer listened intently while he outlined his concerns over her religious views on vengeance and her disdain for BJ.

When he finished, she sat silently for a moment, processing. Then she asked, "This lady admitted nothing, right? This is your gut talking?"

"Yeah," he admitted.

"Well," she conceded, "As long as we have been investigating, we have surprisingly good internal compasses guiding us on who is truthful and who is not. But I want to make sure that you are not judging her on her beliefs instead of facts."

Daniel measured her words thoughtfully. "You know, Jennifer, I don't think so. A couple of times when I mentioned Carrie, she seemed scared."

"Okay. Then how do you address the timeline and the fact that Carrie was alive and well when she left the Katz home?"

"That's the piece I am struggling with."

"Do you want some advice?" she offered.

"Sure, two heads are better than one."

"Go home. You have worked late the last couple of nights. Jason is safe. There's nothing we can do now for Carrie. It's early afternoon; maybe drive to Fairhope and walk on the pier. In other words, let it all go for today."

"Is my supervisor telling me to play hooky?" he looked amused.

"It's not hooky when you have worked back-o-back twelve-hour days. It's called Self-Care. Come back in the morning and review your notes and timeline with fresh eyes. I guarantee you that things will be clearer."

He rose and took their trash. "I will put these in the break room trash, so you won't have to smell fried chicken all afternoon."

"That is very thoughtful. Will you follow my advice?"

He turned back, "It's good advice, so do you mind me giving some back?"

Her eyes narrowed. "Why does that sentence frighten me?"

"Jennifer, you are always on us to care for ourselves, but do you? You come in early. You work late. You skip meals. How can I follow your advice when you don't?"

"As a matter of fact, Mr. Know it all," she said. "I am leaving on time today as well. I have to meet the maintenance man at my apartment. The air conditioner froze up last night. And, despite the fact that we have entered November, I cannot sleep in a hot apartment. "

"Try not to party too hard." His sarcasm was not wasted.

Jennifer held up her hands in mock surrender. "Okay, okay, you are right. I need to follow my own advice. And I will. But right now, with two high-profile cases, the state is constantly on me for updates. When things die down, I will let my hair down."

"We'll see. Maybe we can get a drink one night when things calm down."

Her breath caught in her throat, but she quickly recovered. "Yes, maybe."

She quickly looked down so that Daniel would not see the flush that rose from her neck. And when she looked up, he was gone.

Jennifer blew out her breath slowly.

What was that? Did he ask me out? Or was he merely being polite?

She reflected on the impossibility of a supervisor-subordinate relationship, wondering if she had encouraged it.

Am I encouraging it because I want something to happen? That's not fair to either one of us.

She shook her head, determined to be more professional around him. But even as she had decided that being with Daniel was impossible, the thought of him caused her traitor lips to form a smile. Thoughts of them together triggered a warm sensation in her chest. Expelling the images took determination, but she forced herself to think clearly, muttering, "It wouldn't work. End of story!"

"Ms. Riley?" a soft, soprano voice called her. "Who are you talking to? End of what story?"

Jennifer broke her reverie to see the unit clerk standing in the open doorway.

"Hi, Linda, don't mind me, just talking to myself. How can I help you?"

"Molly called me from downstairs. There is a lady downstairs in the lobby to see you. Says her name is Deena Monroe."

Jennifer sat straight up in her chair. "Deena Monroe? What does she want with me?"

"Well, she didn't rightly say it, but she did tell Molly it was important and private."

"Give me a few minutes, Linda. I wasn't prepared to see her today and need to take care of a couple of things first. Put her in interview room 6 and tell her I will be down in about 15 minutes."

Linda nodded. "Yes, ma'am." "I'll go deliver the message."

Jennifer felt a wave of grief slam into her chest as the thought of talking to Candy's mother reopened the unhealed wound.

How can she face me after all she's done?

Shutting my office door for privacy, she leaned back, her head cradling the leather headrest of the chair. Jennifer closed her eyes and took in a long, slow breath through her nose, held it, and then slowly blew it out through her mouth. Vagal Breathing–an effective tool for relieving anxiety–had been the secret to Jennifer's ability to handle stress. This session lasted about five minutes before Jennifer felt the calm return to her mind. One more slow breath, she opened her eyes and nodded.

Let's go see what Deena Monroe has to say for herself.

20

Deena Monroe sat rigidly on the microfiber chair in Interview Room Six, swiping away on her cell phone as she played Candy Crush. When Jennifer walked in, the woman barely looked up, so intent was she to line up the brightly colored candy pieces and clear the board. Her concentration on the game allowed Jennifer to settle behind the interview desk and appraise the woman.

At 5'5", Jennifer was about 3 inches taller than her visitor and about 50 pounds lighter. Deena, short and square-bodied, wore a perpetual frown—"like she was smelling cabbage,"– as Jennifer's daddy used to say. The older woman's coppery red hair was cut into a short, shaggy style that exaggerated her round face.

As if aware of the scrutiny, Deena looked up from her phone and met Jennifer's gaze. "Ms. Riley, I hope you don't mind, but I had to finish up the game, or else I would lose it."

Jennifer shook her head. "No problem. Although I must admit, I am a little curious as to why you are here today."

Without a word, Deena lifted the sleeve of her long-sleeve tee to reveal deep purple fingerprint marks across her upper arms. "I just wanted you to see what my life was like, and maybe you'd see I ain't such a bad mom."

"Bad mom?" Jennifer spoke slowly, incredulously. But her thoughts were racing.

Bad mom? You win the award for the worst mom.

But her face remained polite.

"You know, I mean about Candy."

"I don't understand what you are getting at." Jennifer wanted to hear where this was leading.

"I know you think it is my fault that my baby girl got herself killed. And maybe it is. God knows I have blamed myself for it ever since it happened. But, Ms. Riley, you only know part of my story. And I think it's time you heard it all."

Jennifer breathed deeply. She realized the Vagal breathing had not resolved the deep anger burning toward Deena over Candy's death. She needed someone to blame, and Candy's family bore the brunt of it. But she also knew that holding onto that anger instead of being open to hearing Deena's truth violated everything she believed in. Jennifer suspected Deena had survived a toxic relationship with her husband. For years she had attempted to get this woman to open up to her. But Deena constructed an emotional concrete wall that Jennifer hadn't been able to penetrate.

She never understood why Candy's mother never stood up for her, protected her, or even gave a damn about her daughter.

"You know, Deena," she began. "You're right. I don't know the whole story. I want to hear it. Please tell me about your family and the side that I don't know."

At first, Deena looked suspicious, trying to gauge whether Jennifer's words were genuine. But after a small pause, she began. "Ms. Riley."

"Call me Jennifer."

"Jennifer, I've been in this area my whole life. As a matter of fact, I was born at home in Chickasaw; my family lived in that housing project there."

"I know the one you are talking about. Go on."

"My daddy worked at one of the mills in Axis: Blastech, and my momma took care of the house. We didn't have much money at all, but we made do. I was raised to believe that the man was the head of the household and the woman's job was to serve her man."

Jennifer understood. Traditional roles for men and women were institutions women from the South battled constantly, especially 40 years earlier.

"My whole family went to the 8 Mile Church of God, where Daddy was a deacon. And he took me to school on his way to work every day so I wouldn't have to ride the bus with the other kids from the project."

"Sounds like you had a good life, Deena. I don't understand."

The woman's lips tightened, emphasizing the puffiness of her cheeks. "Yeah, sounds like I had a good life." She snorted.

"But things weren't as they seemed," Jennifer was beginning to understand.

"I was Daddy's little girl. My momma sometimes yelled at me about being his favorite–his princess. But I didn't feel like no princess."

"Do you want to tell me about it? "Jennifer's voice softened.

"Those days when daddy brought me to school early, well, it wasn't out of the kindness of his heart, let's just say. He would drive me out to one of those gravel pits and, you know, make me do things. Things a little girl ought not to do, especially with their daddy. Then, he'd tell me to wash my face and stop crying. He'd drive me right to school and give me an extra quarter for ice cream as if nothing happened."

"I understand," said Jennifer. "Your daddy abused you sexually."

Deena nodded. "I hated it! I felt myself dying little by little on the inside every time. Pretty soon, I felt like a dead leaf, and if you squeezed me, I would crumble up and blow away." As she spoke, a solitary tear trekked down her round face.

Jennifer got up from the desk and sat next to the broken woman, taking her hand. She had worked with so many sexually abused teens and knew Deena wasn't fabricating the story. Her words rang too true, too similar to other victims. "Go on. Did you tell your mother?"

Deena gave a wry laugh. "Yeah. And you know what she said to me? You wanted to be his princess? Well, how do you like it now?" The tears of a deep, hidden pain started flowing freely.

Jennifer wrapped her arm around her; no longer was she Candy's mom. She was Deena Monroe, a child no one had bothered to see or hear so many years ago.

Deena seemed to regain composure, dabbing her eyes with a Kleenex. "I need to tell you more. I want you to know about Candy."

Jennifer nodded. "Go ahead, Deena."

"I got pregnant with Candy when I was about 15. She is my girl, no doubt. But I wasn't married. I didn't even have a boyfriend. Daddy wouldn't let me be around any other boys. He warned me to stay away from the dirty little peckers."

Jennifer's eyes widened with clarity. "You mean, your daddy is the father of Candy." The information was startling. She had worked with incest victims, even those who became pregnant by their abusers. But she hadn't thought the cold, distant Mrs. Monroe could have been one of them.

Deena smiled weakly, but the effect was unpleasant, like the smiles on antique dolls–cold and sinister. Her attempt to mask the remembered pain failed.

"Yep. Guilty," she said.

"No, Deena, you listen to me. You are not guilty. I need to interject one thing before you go on. What your daddy did to you was not your fault. You did nothing to entice him. He was the adult when he hurt you. He knew better. Please understand that."

"That's not what my momma said when she found out I was pregnant. She called me a whore and a home wrecker. Then she kicked me out of the house."

"Oh, no. Deena. Where did you go?"

"I stayed with our preacher and his wife until I had Candy. At first, I couldn't believe how nice they were to me. They didn't call me names or seem even to judge me. They helped me to get on Medicaid and the WIC and started the ADC paperwork. Of course, they didn't know anything about Daddy's part."

"You never told them who the father was? Were you afraid they would judge you? Or not believe you?"

"Not because of any of that. I was so ashamed. It'd be better if they thought I was a whore."

"So, unaware of your situation, they took you in?"

"Yeah, I was mighty grateful until I found out why."

Jennifer was confused. "What do you mean? Why did they?"

"Once Candy was born, they came to me in the hospital with a social worker like you. That lady, I will never forget her name, Mrs. Harrison, told me I needed to give my baby to the preacher and his wife."

"Give her to them? You mean let them adopt her?"

"She said that because I was only 15, I was gonna have to go into foster care, and that wasn't no place for my baby to grow up. So I needed to sign over my rights."

"And why do you think the preacher and his wife were behind it?" Jennifer knew she should just let the story flow, but the investigator in her kept interrupting.

"Well, when the social worker lady left, I begged them to take me in their home with Candy so I could raise her. And the preacher man said he was sorry, but that Candy would be better away from me and my lifestyle. He told me that he was the one who called the Child Welfare."

"Deena, no wonder you have trouble trusting anyone. And now I understand your distrust of social workers. What did you do?"

"I waited until they brought me candy to feed. Then, when the nurses left, I snuck out of the hospital and hid."

With electronic surveillance and monitoring of the newborns, Jennifer knew that what Deena described would be almost impossible now. But twenty years ago, it could have happened.

Deena continued. "I made it to my Aunt Sil's house in Prichard. Aunt Sil was my momma's sister, but two women were never more different than those two. She never married and always said she wasn't gonna serve no man."

Jennifer grinned. "I think I might have liked Aunt Sil."

Deena continued, "Sil didn't want to get in no trouble, but she felt sorry for me. She let me stay there for almost a year. I worked in her plant nursery and just kept to the house."

Jennifer took in a breath. "Deena, that is quite a lot. I cannot imagine what it was like for you. But it does sound like you finally got someone to help you."

"Yeah," the woman agreed. "Aunt Sil was cool. She smoked a little pot but didn't do any of the hard stuff. I would say she was the nicest person in my family. I liked working in the nursery during the day. At night, she would help me take care of Candy. You know why I named her Candy?"

Jennifer shook her head. "Why?"

When I first got to Aunt Sil's, she didn't have a name. I really couldn't think of anything to call her. I wasn't even sure I liked her."

"That's understandable in your circumstance. Plus, you might have been dealing with some post-partum depression."

"I don't know about all that. But I was always craving chocolate. Aunt Sil kept a lot of Hershey's and stuff around for when she got the munchies; I loved it. Aunt Sil said she would think I was a candy-a-holic if she didn't know better. So I just liked the sound of that. And I decided to call my girl Candy."

Jennifer laughed. "Interesting way to name a child. How did you meet Mr. Munroe?

Deena's smile vanished. "Clyde worked at the nursery too. Part-time, on his days off. His real job was at the cement factory. I met him when I was sixteen. He was a bit older, almost twenty-eight, then. Man, oh man, was he the charmer too. Didn't seem to mind Candy at all. We started dating, you know, off and on for about a year. Even then, he had a little temper on him. I'd break up with him when he would go off on me. Then he would come around with flowers and a lot of "I'm sorry," and I would take him back. What a stupid little girl I was."

Jennifer interjected again, "You're not stupid, Deena. That love-violence pattern had been a way of life for you since you were a child. "

"We up and got married when I turned seventeen. In Alabama, back then, I was old enough."

Jennifer knew that some parents still allowed their teens to get married. She didn't understand it, but she knew it occurred. "Tell me about your life with Mr. Munroe."

"At first, married life was fun. He liked to party and have a good time, and so did I. We would leave Candy at Aunt Sil's house and go to Gulf Shores for days–drinking, sleeping on the beach, and being young and free. I mean, there were times when I still saw the meanness in him. You know? He would get mad when I said something stupid and slap me. But he would always be so sorry. He would beg me not to make him do it again."

Deena described the familiar cycle of domestic violence. The abuser always convinced the victim of her culpability in the violence, feigning remorse and promising redemption. Jennifer waited for Deena to continue.

"Then things got strange. Clyde moved us to a little farm in Citronelle, away from everyone. He wouldn't let me talk to the neighbors, even to Aunt Sil. She tried to come to see me once, but he shooed her off with a shotgun, so she never came back. It got so lonely there that I thought about just taking Candy, leaving, and returning to my aunt."

"But you didn't?"

"Before I could get the nerve up to leave, I found out I was pregnant with Clyde, Jr. Candy was only four, and I knew I couldn't take care of a little one and a teeny baby alone. So I stayed and tried to be a good wife and not make him mad. A couple of years later, my youngest boy was born, and by then, I was truly trapped.."

Jennifer had to ask. "When did you find out he was sexually abusing Candy?" She saw Deena flinch as if slapped. But she slowly nodded.

"I was getting to that," her eyes would not meet Jennifer's. "Not until Candy was about 11. She came to me and told me that her daddy had touched her privates. I went to Clyde and pitched a fit. He denied it, but I demanded that he stop and not touch my little girl ever again, or I would go to the cops."

"But he didn't."

Deena looked down at her hands, and Jennifer saw she was shaking. "That day, he hit me so hard, he broke out two of my teeth. He pulled me around the house by my hair as I screamed for help."

"Sounds like you were scared to intervene?"

"No, weren't that. I would have taken that beating and more to save Candy from what I went through. But then he went into my boys' bedroom, where they were sleeping, and put a gun to both of their heads just to show me that he could. He told me that if I ever told what he did to Candy, he would blow their brains out, and Candy's too."

"Deena!" gasped Jennifer.

"I could take it when he just hurt me, but that night, I realized that Clyde was crazy, and I believed he would kill all my kids."

"When Candy finally told the secret to her teacher, I got you all alone to ask you what you knew. You denied everything and kept quiet. You even blamed Candy for lying."

A strange look came over her face as she said, "I had to lie. Don't you see? I knew you would take Candy away, and I was so relieved. I wouldn't have to worry about her if she got out of that house. But had I confirmed what I knew, I genuinely believe Clyde would have killed me and the boys."

Jennifer didn't educate the grieving mother on the ripple effect of her actions. She didn't want to add to her pain by telling her that Candy, abandoned in her mind by her mother, struggled all her life with self-worth, self-love, and guilt. Sometimes, the truth serves no purpose.

"Deena, thank you for sharing this with me. I cannot tell you how sorry I am for all of the pain you have endured your entire life. It really helps me to understand some of your reasons for the actions and decisions you made."

The other woman relaxed her face. "Jennifer, I may never have told you, but you helped Candy so much. I know Candy did so well because of you."

Jennifer's eyes registered her own grief, which had resurfaced after listening to Candy's mother. "I am just so sorry that it wasn't enough to keep Candy from harm."

Deena shook her head. "You just told me not to blame myself and that we sometimes put ourselves right back into the patterns we know. Didn't you say something like that?"

In amazement, Jennifer realized that the woman to whom she had previously only felt anger was actually trying to comfort her. "Thank you, Deena."

"I mean, if you really think about it, Candy took up with a man like Clyde and my daddy. I wonder if you can ever really get away?"

Jennifer asked. "Yes, Deena. It is possible, but it takes a lot of courage and even more support. I might not have predicted what happened to Candy, but will you let me help you, Deena?

Surprise sprang in her eyes, Deena said. "Help me with what?"

"Your boys are out of the house now. Clyde is still hurting you. Will you let me help you break free?"

Deena faced Jennifer squarely and said with a hollow chord, "I will never be free. Clyde has a bad heart and diabetes. He is having his foot cut off next week. I can't leave him now."

Jennifer felt sick. But after years of working with women who had endured life-long abuse, she knew that until the victim was ready, there would be no persuading her. She gave Deena her card.

"Keep this in a safe place. When and if you ever feel ready to take the step, I will help you. I have resources and people who can keep you safe and help you start a new life. Please call me."

Sadness and weariness returned to Deena's round face as she whispered, "Thank you, Ms. Riley." Then she got up from the chair and left the building.

21

Chris

The boy finished the orange Jell-O, using his fingers to pick up the jiggly bits that fell from his spoon and onto the plastic dinner plate. Orange Jell-O was the bomb, though. Who knew? At his house, they had only had strawberry or lime, Billy's favorite. But now? Orange was going to be his favorite flavor!

"Chris?" he heard Michael's voice as the social worker–his social worker, he reminded himself with pride–walked into the room.

"How ya doing, buddy? I had to go down the hall to finish some notes and make some calls. But I bet you missed me, right?"

Chris smiled. "Nah. Karen came by, and she is nicer and prettier than you."

Michael grabbed his chest and groaned. "You hurt me now. I am wounded. He pretended to fall against the door, smiling at the sound of Chris' laughter. He could not believe the resiliency of that kid, laughing spontaneously; after all, he had been through.

"Look who's got jokes now?" Michael chided him good-naturedly.

"I didn't really hurt your feelings, did I?" the boy asked, uncertain about whether he should apologize.

"Michael waved his hand, "Pfft. I can take a joke. Besides, Karen is prettier than me."

The boy shrugged, and Michael said, "I have some news for you. Do you want to hear it?"

The boy nodded quickly.

"My supervisor, Ms. Jennifer, talked with your dad today. He came all the way to Mobile to make sure you were okay."

Chris' eyes widened. "He did? Where is he? Is he going to come to see me?"

"Slow down there, hoss. Give me time to get it out of my mouth." Michael winked at Chris.

"Yes, he is still in town, and yes, he is going to come to the hospital to see you in a couple of hours—around 7 o'clock."

"Is he mad at me?" Chris didn't even want to think about it, but he remembered how his daddy and momma were before Billy died.

Michael pulled the chair up to the bed. "Of course, he is not mad with you. He is mad with himself."

"Why? What did he do?"

"Well, Chris, he feels bad that he was living in another town while your mom was hurting you."

"I don't understand. It wasn't his fault. Why does he feel bad?"

"Well, son, as a father, he blames himself for not trying harder to contact you. Your mother wasn't answering the phone when he called, and he feels like he should have tried harder."

"I wish he hadn't left. But I am not mad at him," Chris said thoughtfully.

"I think he would really like it if you told him that. You know, Chris, most of all, He wishes he had taken you with him."

"He does?" Chris looked unbelieving.

"Yes, he does. And he wants to take you back with him when you get out of the hospital."

"He does?" Chris repeated.

Michael tousled the sandy hair. "Yes, he does."

They both looked up when they heard another knocking on the open door. Standing in the doorway, looking lost, was Chris' father, Ken Barry. He walked into the hospital room almost timidly, eyes locked on his son in the bed. Chris watched him wordlessly, his mouth a perfectly round O as Mr. Barry approached the bedside. He stood awkwardly as if he had no idea what to do next.

Michael recovered first. "Mr. Barry, Hi. I thought you were coming at seven tonight."

Reaching out for Chris' hand, Mr. Barry replied. "I couldn't wait until seven. I wanted to make sure my boy was alright."

"Daddy. You came to see me." Chris whispered.

Mr. Barry bent down, scooping the boy in a tight bear hug. "Oh, Chris, of course, I came to see you."

"I am so sorry!" he said. "I didn't know what your mom was doing. I promise you I would have come sooner."

Chris said, "It's okay, Daddy. You came now."

Michael relinquished his chair by the bed so that Mr. Barry could sit. Chris held his father's hand like it was a lifeline. They sat together in silence for several moments but never broke eye contact. Michael found the scene mesmerizing. He watched for a while and then felt intrusive, so he quietly excused himself to leave the room.

Mr. Barry broke the silence first. "I talked to your doctor. He said that you should be able to be released tomorrow. That means they will let you go home."

Fear slowly crept into Chris' face as he repeated, "Home?"

Understanding, his father quickly explained. "Not to that house. Never again to that house. I'll sell it, so you never have to go there again."

"Where will I go?" he was confused. "Do I have to go live with that family Michael told me about?"

Mr. Barry squeezed his hand. "No, son. You are going to live with me in Gulf Shores. I live about a mile from the beach. When it's warm, we can go swimming and build sandcastles."

"Can we go to the beach as soon as we get to your house? It's warm now."

Mr. Barry laughed. "Not warm enough for the beach, silly. And it is our house; I want you to feel like you belong there, with me."

Chris smiled. "What about the family I was supposed to go live with?"

"I talked with Ms. Riley, who is Michael's supervisor. She fixed it so when you leave the hospital, you get to come home with me to live."

"Forever?"

Mr. Barry chuckled. "Well, you won't want to live there forever once you become an adult. But yes, as long as you want!"

Chris grinned, feeling a sense of relief and peace he had not felt in a long time. But a nagging thought still bothered him. "But where will momma go when her head sickness gets better?"

"When she gets well enough to get out of the hospital, son, she still has to take responsibility for the bad things she did. She might not need anywhere to live for a long time. But if she does, I will help her find her own place."

"Is she going to jail?" his face looked sad.

"I don't know," his father answered honestly. "If not jail, she will need some long-term treatment. She was sicker than I ever knew. And that was my fault."

Chris shook his head. "Not your fault."

But his father sighed. "When I think of all the signs I missed, all the things I should have put together over the years, I think I would have known. But I was so happy... with her, with you, with Billy. It wasn't until we lost your brother that she wasn't able to hide her sickness any longer."

Chris watched as his father started crying. He had never seen his dad cry, and, as he thought about it, he had never seen any adult cry. It was strange.

"Daddy?" he nudged his father's hand until he got his attention.

Wiping his eyes, Mr. Barry answered, "Yes, son?"

"What does the Easter Bunny drive?"

The man's face, so sad a second ago, drew blank. "What?"

"The Easter Bunny."

"I don't know what you are talking about, son."

"The Easter Bunny drives a Volkswagen Rabbit!"

Mr. Barry started laughing softly, building into a release of tension until he was laughing so hard that the tears came anyway. With a heart of unbelievable gratefulness at his good fortune, he took the boy into his arms again.

22

Daniel

The next morning, Daniel was back on the steps of the Ossie porch, knocking. Instead of Brian, BJ opened the door.

"BJ, I'm glad to see you. I wasn't sure whether or not you would be back."

Her face, sallower than the first time he had seen her, had been ravaged by spent tears and grief. Daniel's heart moved at the sight of the woman's apparent internal pain.

She replied in a flat voice, "They let me go to plan for Carrie's funeral. Detective Green said he would need to talk to me again soon. "

When he didn't reply immediately, she said, "Mr. Daniel, I know you don't believe me. Nobody does. But the police finally told me what killed my little girl. They said someone shook her so hard that her brain rattled back and forth in her brain. Is that true?"

"That's what caused her brain to swell and for her to die, yes."

"You need to know. I didn't shake Carrie. I didn't. God as my witness, I didn't. I put her to bed as soon as I got home, and when I woke up, she wasn't breathing. That's God's truth." She made the sign of the cross on her chest.

Despite the sincerity in her denial, Daniel challenged her. "BJ, you had done drugs that night. How can you remember what you did and didn't do?"

"Yes," she admitted calmly. "I did smoke pot that night, and I took some Lortabs. But I didn't do meth or horse on account of Jason being with me. I should've told you, but I knew you wouldn't believe me.

But, Mr. Daniel, I have thought about it over and over and over; I remember everything that happened."

"And?"

"And I didn't shake my little girl."

Daniel considered her passionate plea. "Remind me about when you picked up Carrie from Miss Katz's house. Was she asleep or awake?"

"She was asleep. Like dead to the world sleep. Oh! That sounds so awful; I didn't mean to say that."

"Well, tell me what you meant. Was she sleeping hard?"

"For sure. She didn't even so much as whimper when I carried her across the street. She don't usually sleep that hard, you know. At first, I felt lucky cuz it meant I could go on to sleep."

"Did anything else seem different?"

"Not that I can remember. I noticed her sleeping hard, but she was breathing fine! I would've done sumpin if she weren't."

"And what time was this?" Daniel prodded.

"As I said."

"Now, BJ, I am trying to help you get to the truth. You told me a couple of things that weren't exactly true. One of them was the time you picked up Carrie. You said around eight or nine, and Miss Katz says around eleven."

BJ lowered her head as she slowly shook it. "Yeah, I guess it was closer to eleven than to eight. I didn't want you to think unkindly toward me, being out so late."

"I just want to know the truth. It will help me figure out some things."

"What things? She looked hopeful. "So you believe me? You don't think I kilt my baby?"

Daniel caught her eye and held the gaze. "BJ, I don't think you knowingly hurt Carrie. And maybe you didn't at all. But I need complete answers so I can figure that out. Will you be straight with me?"

She nodded, her bottom lip trembling.

"You picked up Carrie at eleven and brought her home, putting her into bed. And she never woke up, never cried?"

"Nah. She just stayed asleep."

Daniel continued. "Brian and Jason were here, but Brian had passed out before you picked up the kids, and Jason went to his own bed."

At her continued nodding, Daniel kept going. "You got up between 2:00 and 3:00 am, right?"

"Yessir."

"Did Carrie cry and wake you up? Or did you get up on your own?"

BJ cocked her head to the side, processing the question. "No, I don't think I heard a peep from her. I just got up to take a pee."

"And when you went into her room, she wasn't breathing."

He saw the tears start to form. "Yes, sir."

"BJ, what made you go into her room if she wasn't crying?"

"I don't rightly know. Something just told me to go check on her."

Daniel felt he was missing something. "And there's nothing else you remember about when you picked her up or after you got home?"

"She was wearing a new little nightgown that Miss Katz had gotten her."

"Did you not send a nightgown with her?"

Irritation flashed briefly in her face. "Of course, I sent a gown with her. I am not such a bad mother."

Then she said quickly," Wait, I remember. Miss Katz told me Carrie had thrown up right before she went to sleep. She thought the baby might be coming down with a bug or something. But like I done said, Carrie was fast asleep when I got her."

Daniel thought for a moment. "Thank you, BJ. I know it's hard to talk about, but you gave me good information. Let's shift gears. Where's Brian?"

Her lips puckered, "That son-bitch is in jail. Cops came and found some meth in his gym bag. So he is waiting for me to bail him out. But that ain't happening. Good riddance to a bad penny."

"That's probably a good idea if you want to help yourself."

"Mr. Daniel, I know I can't blame him for me messing up again, but damn it, I had been clean for so long."

"What are you going to do now BJ?"

"The social worker for Jason told me about a Woman's Rehab in Birmingham. It's called Alethia House. I wanted to leave Mobile, and the social worker said this is a good place."

"I'm glad to see you are getting help again, BJ.."

"I know as long as they think I killed Carrie, they will never give me Jason back. But I keep praying someone believes me one day. And when that day comes, I need to be clean and on my feet so I can try and get Jason back."

Daniel said, "I know Jason misses you, so it's a good picture to remember when you're working the program."

"Mr. Daniel, will I get to see Jason? He doesn't know what's happening. He is lost as a little lamb right now."

Daniel softened his voice. "I will arrange for supervised visitation for you two this week. But BJ, you must show you are serious about getting and staying clean if you want him back for good."

"I know, Mr. Daniel. He's all I got left."

Daniel rose to leave and promised the young mother he would talk to her that week about the visitation.

Once in his car, he called Carol Blessing. She answered quickly and curtly. He smiled at her usual cursory greeting.

He talked with her about some of his suspicions around the death of Carrie Ossie, specifically listing a few questions that he wanted her to ask Dr. Lambert. She agreed and told him she would contact him with the information.

As he backed out of the Ossie drive, he noticed Miss Katz watching him from her stoop where she had been sweeping. He caught her eye and offered a quick wave of his hand. However, she behaved as if she hadn't seen him and hastily returned to her planned task.

23

Jennifer and Daniel

Daniel, craving a cup of dark roast coffee, walked into Starbucks and ordered a Vente. He was about to exit the store with his prize when he spotted Jennifer sitting alone at a corner table, eating a scone. She had her hand on a cup of coffee and her face on the Mobile Press/Register sports page from the previous Sunday and had not noticed his presence in the shop.

"You know your paper is a few days old," he joked.

Folding down a corner of the page, she peered at him. "I only read the Sunday paper," she retorted. "And if you hadn't noticed, this week has been busy. This is my first chance to catch up on the SEC."

"Mind if I join you?"

When she didn't immediately reply, he offered, "I can go if you want privacy."

"No," she waved him into a chair. "I finished the article. We have to pull out all the tricks to beat LSU this Saturday. Auburn already has two losses this year, so LSU is the only team in our way toward winning the SEC West!"

"Of course, we will beat those corndogs," he laughed. "They have the cookie monster as their coach."

Jennifer laughed loudly. Although she had not verbalized it, she had also thought the LSU coach's voice sounded like the Sesame Street character. There was no denying that Coach Orgeron knew what he was doing, as he had really whipped that LSU team into shape. But Jennifer had to strain to understand his words every time he opened his mouth.

"Aren't you from Louisiana? I thought you'd be my football rival?"

Daniel put his hand across his heart in mock disbelief. "Are you profiling me? I have you know, even in Louisiana, I was a Green Wave fan."

She chuckled. "Tulane? You are a social worker. Always pulling for the underdogs."

He laughed and shrugged. "What can I say?"

Jennifer's smile widened. "Well, any enemy of LSU is a friend of mine!" she declared.

Daniel began sipping his coffee while Jennifer put away her paper and started tackling the scone with relish. "What's going on with Michael's little boy now?" he asked.

Jennifer filled him in on Michael's case with the boy from the basement. She mentioned that the case was headed toward a happy conclusion. Although Chris had made a full physical recovery and would be going home with his dad, he would most likely need intensive mental health follow-up. Trauma was a tricky thing. The ordeal that the little boy endured created some scars, even if they did not show up yet. According to Jennifer, his father had already made appointments for a child psychologist in Gulf Shores to assess the boy. The case would be transferred to the Baldwin County DHR so that they could follow the family and add other support to them as well.

Daniel felt a sense of warmth begin in his chest and travel down his limbs. He attributed it, at first, to the coffee. However, as he observed Jennifer talking animatedly about the case, he knew it was something else. Her eyes shone brightly, and her entire face seemed to glow as she recounted details.

Damn, she is beautiful.

"Dealing with trauma daily takes such a toll; it's nice to hear a good outcome once in a while," she finished.

"Did they ever find out if the mom poisoned him?" asked Daniel.

"They did find Celexa in his system," she replied. "Mom hadn't meant to kill him—at least not at that time. She just wanted to knock him out so she could play Halloween. Unfortunately, the dose almost killed him because his little system did not have any food in it to absorb the meds."

Daniel whistled. "What happens to her now?"

Jennifer shook her head. "Daniel, that lady is deeply disturbed. She won't be discharged anytime soon. Just means Chris and his dad will have plenty of time to rebuild their bond together. In the end, I believe Chris will be okay. Michael says he is super resilient.

Daniel's eyes sharpened on Jennifer's face, noticing a wistfulness began to transform her features. He knew her mind went to Candy as she continued to navigate that loss. He wanted to comfort his supervisor.

Not just supervisor. Friend.

Despite the work-dynamic, Daniel found himself caring about Jennifer, and he could tell she was still not herself. He wanted to ask her about it but decided to be patient.

She'll talk when she's ready.

Instead, Daniel updated Jennifer about the Ossie case and his talk with BJ.

"So you don't think Mom did it?" she probed.

"You know, Jennifer. I don't. I know there's nobody else in the timeline when the child died, but I don't think she did it."

He told her about his call to Carol Blessing. "I am waiting for Carol to call back, and if she confirms my research, then we might be able to prove BJ didn't shake Carrie."

Jennifer said, "You are like a dog with a bone. When I am ever accused of murder, I want you to investigate!"

"Not if you did it; you don't," he smiled a toothy grin. "I'll bust you."

"I bet you would, she shot back. And they laughed together.

"So what are you doing this weekend for fun?" asked Daniel.

"Watching the game, of course!" she looked at him in disbelief. "What else would I be doing? Hello? LSU?"

"I am having some friends over Saturday for a cook-out by the lake and you can bet we will be watching the game too. Want to come?"

Her smile froze. "I mean, sure, I'd love to. It sounds like fun."

"I am sensing a but," he said.

"But I just think it would look bad. What would people think? I am your supervisor, and even with a group of friends, it could look inappropriate." Her crooked smile did not mask her disappointment.

Daniel smiled. "Normally, I would say, who gives a damn what people think. But I get it. Don't want the hens and roosters to talk. Well, too bad. Cause you're right! It would have been fun."

Jennifer rose and threw away her cup and plate. "Well, you may live a life of leisure, but I have to get back to the rat race. See you at the office."

But before he could answer, the phone rang. He said quickly, "It's Carol." And he strode out of the coffee shop. She heard, "Daniel Bradshaw," before the door closed behind him.

24

Daniel

Daniel stared once again at the yellow door with the burlap cross and knocked rapidly. There was no sound of the television like last time. But within a few minutes, he heard her call out.

"Yes? Who is it?"

"Miss Katz, it's Daniel Bradshaw from DHR. Remember we talked before? About Carrie Ossie?"

The door opened to a vastly different Ida Mae Katz. She wore a long, white terrycloth robe cinched at the waist. Disheveled hair covered her face like a veil. The difference was alarming.

"Miss Katz, are you alright? Are you coming down with something?" the social worker asked, concerned.

She seemed to have aged overnight. However, she slowly opened the door and walked with a slow shuffle, waving him into the kitchen.

"Are you sick?" he repeated the question.

"No, dear. I am just feeling my age," she replied. "I was about to have my afternoon cup of coffee. Would you join me?"

"I just finished a large coffee a bit ago. I better hold off on the caffeine. But please go ahead and make your cup. I will wait at the table if that's okay with you."

She didn't answer, which he took as consent. She padded into the kitchen as he sat at the table, still decorated for guests who never came. Returning with a mug of black coffee, she had a long drink before speaking.

"How can I help you now, Mr. Bradshaw?"

"I wanted to go back over your time with Carrie on the night she died, if that's okay. I am finalizing my report and want to ensure I have all the important information."

Looking deeply into her cup, she replied, "I am not sure what else I can tell you other than what I have already said."

"Well, I have a few different questions. You know, there are things I didn't think of when I was here."

"Fine."

Daniel glanced at his notes and asked, "Was Carrie a fussy baby normally? I mean, would she have given her mother or Brian grief at night?"

Miss Katz smiled wearily, "All babies can be fussy, Mr. Bradshaw. Do you have any children of your own?"

He shook his head. "No, ma'am. I don't."

"Well," she began schooling him. "Babies get fussy for all kinds of reasons. Their little tummies bother them when they have gas; they fuss when they are hungry or even when they are just bored. So a mother gets used to handling a fussy baby."

"How did BJ handle Carrie when she was fussy?"

"I don't know. I didn't socialize with the family."

Daniel wrote her words like a student in the class. "So Carrie was fussy like other babies but not more so. Is that what you are saying?"

"Well, you know, Carrie could be a touch annoying from time to time. She liked to cling to me. Yes, I would say she was a bit needy. But I just chalked it up to her mother and that so-called boyfriend not giving her the right amount of attention."

"I bet that a fussy baby can be annoying," agreed Daniel. "But you know, Miss Katz, you never had kids; how do you know what to do or how to handle it when babies are annoying?"

The wariness returned as her face tightened. "I handle it as my momma taught me, of course. I walk the baby, burp it, change it, or whatever it needs to stop fussing."

"That sounds exhausting," interjected Daniel. "You must be a saint to put up with all of that for a baby that is not yours. And even worse, a baby whose mother uses drugs."

"It is exhausting," she agreed. "And I do it because it is my charitable duty as a Christian. That baby can't help that her mother was a sorry woman. No, sir, it wasn't Carrie's fault. But I do think that her momma's drug-using is what made her so dad-gum fussy."

Then Daniel knew for certain he was on the right track.

"And that night?" he asked.

"What do you mean?"

"Was she extra fussy that night?"

"Who says she was?" the woman asked quickly.

"No-one. I was just asking. Maybe she was sick that night?"

Miss Katz jumped on the word. "Yes, I think she was. She seemed to have a ton of gas and colic. She cried and fussed most of the night."

"And you were walking and rocking, and I bet you even sang to her to make her happy."

"I did. I sang her gospel songs from my church."

"But no matter what you did, she kept fussing like some ungrateful child."

"She sure did! She would not stop crying no matter what I did."

"You really tried, didn't you? You fed her, changed her, and tried everything your momma taught you, but even then, she never stopped crying."

Daniel saw tears forming in the old woman's eyes, which stirred his compassion. But kept going.

"So, at your wit's end, after trying everything else, you shook her. You shook her to get her to stop crying."

Ida Mae Katz folded into herself. The trickle of tears became a deluge, and her shoulders shook with sobs. "I did. I did. I shook her. Just one time, but I shook her hard. I thought I could shock her into stopping."

Empathy gripped Daniel as he watched the broken woman before him.

"And did it? Did the crying stop?"

"Yes. She stopped crying. Her eyes got wide, and she just looked at me. But a few minutes later, she started throwing up. I didn't know what to do."

"What happened then, Miss Katz?"

"I cleaned her up, gave her some water, and rocked her. Eventually, she fell asleep. She was still asleep when BJ came to pick her up. But Mr. Bradshaw, she was alive when she left my house. She was alive."

"I know," he replied. Daniel took a second before sharing the news that he knew would devastate the older woman.

"She was alive, gasped Miss Katz. "So I couldn't have killed her.

Daniel put his hand on hers, and she didn't pull away. "I don't think you meant to harm Carrie at all," he spoke quietly. "But you did."

She turned her delicate hand around and gripped his as if to absorb his strength. Her eyes grew alarmed as he continued. "I talked to the doctor at the hospital. Traumatic Brain Injury caused by the sudden shaking of an infant can have a delayed manifestation. The throwing up and the deep sleep made me wonder if my timeline was off. I found out from the hospital that the injury leading to her desk could have happened many hours earlier."

Her eyes were still moist, but all of the light had gone out of them. With a flat, emotionless tone, Miss Katz said, "Then it was me. Not BJ, not that drug addict, but me."

"Yes, ma'am. It was," he responded.

"I didn't mean to hurt the little thing." Her voice trembled.

"I know."

Several minutes passed while she stared at one of the framed needlepoints on her dining wall- the one that said God is Always Watching. Finally, she breathed out a ragged breath and faced Daniel. "So what do I do now?"

"Unfortunately, I have to report my findings to the police, and they will also want to talk to you. I am sorry."

He had expected her to react, but all she did was nod. "I understand."

Daniel added, "They will take into consideration your age and your intent, which was not to harm the child. But I want to be honest with you. There will be consequences."

She rose, and he took his cue, rising also. As they walked toward the door, she smiled weakly, "I killed an innocent baby. I deserve more consequences than they can give. Thank you for coming and telling me the truth."

Daniel bid her goodbye and walked to his car. All the self-righteousness she displayed on his first visit had been replaced by remorse. The truth emerged from the chaos of circumstance, but at what cost?

The whole damn thing feels like a tragedy.

He called Jennifer, alerting her to the visit and Miss Katz's confession. She listened sympathetically, as she could hear from Daniel's voice that it was a hard visit.

"Listen, Daniel, I know it's the end of the day, but if you want to come by the office and talk about it, I'll be here until around 6:00."

"I might just take you up on that," he replied. "I still have to let Detective Green know that Miss Katz is the one who shook Carrie. He will want to question her. But first, I am going to tell Ms. Ossie that she didn't kill her baby."

25

Jennifer

As the end of the day drew near, Jennifer wondered what had happened to Daniel. She glanced at her Fitbit and noticed that it was 6:00 p.m.

Should I wait? It seemed he needed to talk. But he never showed up.

She examined the underlying emotion lingering in the back of her mind. It was disappointment. She had to admit that she looked forward to talking with Daniel again.

The realization made her extremely nervous. She could not allow herself to harbor anything other than professional feelings for her subordinate. Not only was it strictly forbidden for supervisors to have non-professional relationships with their staff, but it was also unwise. Jennifer remembered the last time she had enjoyed a serious romantic relationship.

At least a couple of years ago, she and Brad were dating. They had been together for almost three years before he had left. His parting words still echoed in her mind.

"Jen, when you find someone you care about more than CPS, I hope you show him."

Maybe Brad had a point.

Those who did not have a calling for child welfare often didn't understand those who did. At least with Daniel, she shared the commitment and drive to do whatever it took to ensure children's safety.

Stop dwelling, Jennifer. It can't happen.

She grew tired of this internal argument. Why fixate on an impossible relationship? Daniel had no desire to become a supervisor or to leave the unit. Therefore, it was up to her to keep everything platonic and professional.

"You still here?" she heard Michael's voice in the doorway.

"No," she retorted. "I am not."

He laughed an easy laugh. "Okay. Well, I had planned to turn in my case to Chris Barry. But since you are not here, I'll just put it in your box."

"Eh, give it here," she reached out with her hand and took the folder. "I will read it tomorrow; my brain can't handle such an intense case tonight. How are you feeling?"

"It was touch and go with my emotions at first," the young investigator admitted.

"That's normal, Michael. You were dealing with some serious trauma."

"I still can't believe it," he said. "The things that the little boy endured at the hands of his own mother."

"It's hard not to let yourself feel angry about things like that. I even had a moment of it when talking to his mom."

"Yeah," he frowned. "You probably handled it better than me."

"I don't know. In the end, we have to acknowledge our feelings of anger, disbelief, and even sometimes disgust."

"What do you mean acknowledge it?" he was puzzled.

"To ourselves," she replied.

"We have to acknowledge to ourselves that we feel these things. If we deny or try to push them down, they'll come out when we don't want them to."

Michael listened.

"Let's take Ms. Barry, for example. While interviewing her, I felt her malice toward that innocent little boy and no remorse for the damage she inflicted on him. Immediately, my curiosity turned to anger."

"I get it. I would feel the same."

"That's the humanity in us–the need for justice. But Ms. Barry needed something far more than justice. Her battle involves a serious mental illness. I reminded myself that she was sick, not evil. "

"But what she did was evil," argued Michael.

"What she did was hurtful and harmful," agreed Jennifer. "But the psychosis led to the behavior, not an intentional desire to cause harm."

"If you say so," Michael frowned.

"Think about it. In her mind, she lost her first child and wanted to protect her second child from a malevolent force that she believed attacked her family. That doesn't excuse anything. It just helps us to understand the 'why'."

"Michael looked thoughtfully at her. "Is it so important to understand the why? Can't I get by just investigating what happened and protecting kids? Not to be funny, but why do I need to know the why?"

Jennifer smiled. "You've been investigating for about a year, right?"

"Eleven months this week!" he corrected.

"Alright, Aubie. I understand you 'plains' people need it broken down. So let's be precise."

"You had to go to football?"

"Can't help myself," she laughed.

Michael rolled his eyes good-naturedly.

"Anyway, she continued. "In eleven months, you've been impressive with your initiative, your innate sense of evidentiary methods, and your analytical mind."

"Really?" he smiled.

"I am going to estimate that you have investigated about 120 different child abuse/neglect cases. Can you remember all of them?"

"No, but I remember some of them."

"Let me take a stab at this," she challenged.

"You remember the ones where children were seriously hurt. And you remember the ones you couldn't substantiate even though you knew the perpetrator."

"You're right."

"And you remember the ones that made no sense to you."

Michael nodded. "I guess you're right there as well.

"Michael, every traumatic case you work on involves you getting to where the child is and understanding their trauma. Once their stories come out of their mouths, a little of the trauma escapes, too, in the form of fear, emotion, and pain. That trauma is passed on to you, and you carry it with you the whole time."

"I don't like the sound of that, " he protested.

"Well, most people in this field don't realize how much secondary trauma they absorb every day."

"I see where you are going, supervisor. But what does that have to do with knowing the why and cutting people slack when they do bad things to kids."

"It's not about cutting people slack," said a deeper male voice.

Jennifer's head spun to see Daniel enter her office. "It's about understanding the cycle of abuse and knowing that hurt people hurt people."

"Hurt people hurt people," repeated Michael slowly. "I like the sound of that. It's easy to understand."

Daniel added, "I didn't mean to jump in on your conversation, but it sounded so interesting, I couldn't help it."

Jennifer motioned toward the other chair in her office. "Come on in. Sit down. We are talking about the Barry case and how Ms. Barry's mental illness played such a big part in the abuse of her child."

She turned back to Michael. "As Daniel said, it's not about cutting anyone slack. Ms. Barry will spend a while in the hospital and possibly in jail for the abuse of Chris. She will face consequences. But as I spoke to her, by understanding that she was sick, I was able to self-talk myself into understanding rather than blame."

"What does it matter? She doesn't care whether you blame her or not," argued the young man.

"You are right. She doesn't. But it goes back to what I was saying about secondary trauma. Acknowledging the feelings and the fact that you took on some of Chris' trauma can help you to find a balance within yourself. I mean, you can't keep the trauma bottled up."

"Is this where that self-care talk you always give us comes in?"

Daniel laughed. "She does, doesn't she? Every monthly meeting."

Jennifer threw up her hands. "I am trying to ensure you don't burn out and leave. Do you know that the turnover for social workers is at 40% in the United States? One of the main reasons is secondary traumatic stress."

Michael nodded. "I get ya. I have had a few days where I wondered if I even wanted to come in the next day."

Daniel nodded. "Everyone has those. But the thing is, you did. And I know you will keep coming in. You got a knack for this job."

"Thanks, man." Michael gave Daniel a fist bump while Jennifer watched them. She smiled at Michael.

"Anyway, I'm sorry I preached at you about self-care. But it is important, and it is important to own your feelings about the tough things we see and hear every day."

"Yes, boss." Michael winked at Daniel and then turned serious. "All joking aside, I felt so protective of Chris, angry at the abuse. But seeing him and his dad together seemed to help–it was a good outcome for the boy."

"Closure is important as well," Jennifer said.

Michael rose to leave. "Oh, boss. Since I turned this case in and have nothing else due this week, can I take some self-care and have Friday off? A long weekend in Pensacola would really help my fragile psyche."

Daniel laughed heartily, and Jennifer smiled. "You are going to milk my good-natured talk for all its worth, right?"

"That's how I roll!"

"Sure, turn in your time sheet and enjoy your long weekend."

He saluted her and left the office.

Daniel's mouth turned up into a wry smile. "Do you remember when you were that green?"

"Actually, I do." She returned the smile. "I remember how some of the cases used to eat me up. I remember the nights of insomnia when I couldn't get the little faces out of my head."

"Hmmm, now that you mention it, me too."

A moment of silence passed before Daniel spoke. "But that doesn't happen anymore, right? You don't still lose sleep over cases? And before you answer that, let me remind you that you are still under oath."

Jennifer threw a mock glare in his direction. "Yeah, busted. So what? Certain cases still stay with me. Why do you think I was trying to talk to Michael about acknowledging his feelings?"

"Me too," he admitted. "As I got older, I thought I had conquered those secondary trauma moments. But listening to your talk with Michael, I realized you were also talking to me."

Jennifer sighed. "We all need to find ways to unloose the extra trauma we carry around. I still haven't let go of the failure I felt when I heard about Candy."

Daniel didn't answer, hoping she would keep going, and was gratified when she did.

"Guess who came to see me today. Don't bother; you will never guess. It was Candy's mom."

"What the hell for?" exclaimed Daniel. "Hadn't she caused enough pain as it is? Was she trying to blame you for her daughter's death?" He could feel anger rising.

"No. Not at all."

Jennifer told Daniel about Mrs. Monroe's visit. She felt a lump in her throat as she recounted the years of systematic abuse that the woman had experienced in her lifetime. Daniel just listened with an occasional question for clarification. After she had finished, he let out a low whistle.

"Often, parents parent as they were parented," he began. "And when a family member molests a child, there is usually sexual abuse in their history. But, damn, that must have been hard to hear."

Jennifer's mouth turned slightly. "The hardest part is knowing how much Mrs. Monroe continues to suffer and being unable to help her at all."

"No. I get it. As an adult, she has the right to make her own choices. You can't force her to get help. But I have been there too, and it made me feel so useless."

"Exactly! Useless! That is how I felt."

"You offered her a branch and your contact information. Maybe one day she will reach out."

"I hope so. I also felt guilty."

"Jennifer, why on earth would you feel guilty?"

"I knew the cycle of abuse and that mothers of children who are molested too often come from trauma themselves. When she first shut me out, I should have pushed harder."

"You told me yourself, Jen, that she purposefully kept the information from you to protect Candy and her brothers. You have got to stop feeling guilty over things beyond your control."

She was momentarily surprised at the emotion in his tone. It was intimate and deeply caring. Not knowing what to feel, she resorted to humor, retorting, "You leave my overactive super-ego out of this!"

"Since we are talking about this, I have another thing to say. I am probably out of line since you are my supervisor, but I wish you would take your own advice."

Jennifer cut her eyes, "What does that mean?"

"You were so good with Michael, helping him to understand secondary trauma. Everything you said was spot on the money."

"Yeah? So?" she didn't know where he was going with this.

Daniel looked at her, his eyes soft and caring. "Jen, you have been carrying around the trauma of Candy's death for a few days now, and it is tearing you up."

Jennifer didn't answer. She didn't have to. Tears once again sprang to her blue-gray eyes. He knew he had hit the nerve.

After several minutes, neither of them spoke a word, but Jennifer said softly, "I know."

"Look, it's nothing to be ashamed of, as you explained to Michael. However, you need to acknowledge it."

Jennifer tried to joke, "Why, sir, are you feeding me my words? They taste like cardboard and ash."

"Why not," he shrugged. "They were great words spoken by a compassionate leader. Why wouldn't I steal them?"

"Her shoulders slumped. "I admit I haven't been myself lately. I feel like my insides are going to explode, and if I let go, I will cry and not be able to stop. Does that sound ridiculous?"

He stretched his arm across the table and took her hand into his. She knew she should pull back; allowing this non-professional gesture was inappropriate. But she didn't. The warmth and strength in his hands soothed her like a warm breeze.

"You know, Jen," he continued, "Ms. Abernathy just started a Secondary Trauma support group."

"She did?" Beverly Abernathy, the Mobile County DHR director, had posted a survey to staff about the support they might need. But she never responded, thinking others needed support more than she did.

"Yes, and it meets weekly. The best thing about it is that it is a drop-in group. Come when you need it, stop when you don't."

"That sounds like an excellent idea, "she admitted. "I wouldn't want to get tied into something that would take even more of my time. I might check it out. What can it hurt?"

"Nothing, he grinned. "Absolutely nothing."

Suddenly, she was conscious again of their hands, and she slowly drew hers out of his. "Thank you, Daniel. Here, I'm supposed to support you, not the other way around.."

His smile was electric. "I am ready when you are."

"And we are back to the jokes."

"Seriously, we are supposed to support each other. And we do. But now, I have to run." He rose and started toward the door.

"Hey!" she called, making him turn back around. "I thought you came here to vent to me?"

Laughing, he shrugged again. "What can I say? It wasn't my turn."

"Daniel, I want to hear about your day. You seemed upset earlier."

"I was. I also learned from Detective Green that he is going to interview Miss Katz tomorrow morning. I feel like she is going to freak out. So I am going with him for moral support for her."

"You're a good guy, Daniel. Your part in this is over, you know."

"I know," he responded. "On paper, it is. But I need to see this through."

"I understand. Then let's talk tomorrow afterward. Maybe you can let me listen to you for a change."

"Sounds like a plan."

She watched as he walked out of her office and followed him with her gaze as he traversed the long corridor leading to the elevator.

What had just happened?

She had to stop pretending that she didn't feel something for Daniel. When he had taken her hand, she didn't want him to let go. Of course, she was attracted to him. He was handsome, kind, intelligent, funny. And she could tell that he felt something for her as well. And when he got her to open up about Candy, she felt safe and protected. The wall she usually put up to hide her feelings from the world came down when they were together. He was, in essence, the man she had been looking for her entire life.

And she could not do anything about it. Everything in her education and training told her she could not pursue this. The flirting had to stop. Furthermore, as the supervisor, she was responsible for getting things back in line with policy and procedure. Something had to be done. She didn't know how she would tell him without being offensive. She would figure it out.

26

Daniel

The clock alarm buzzed simultaneously with his cell phone. Groaning, Daniel rolled over, hit the button on the first, and spoke gruffly into the second.

"Hello?" his graveling voice told volumes of the rough night he had spent the night before. After scolding Jennifer about letting things keep her up at night, he had insomnia for most of the night. But it wasn't a case that kept him up. It was Jennifer. The thought of her and the wanting of her bombarded his thoughts until he finally fell into a troubled sleep around 4:00 am. And now the phone put an end to whatever rest he would get.

"Hello?" he said again into the receiver. He heard ragged breathing. "Who is this?"

"Mr. Daniel?" the voice was soft and breathless.

"Yes, who is this?" he demanded.

"It's... it's BJ. BJ Ossie. Remember, you gave me your number and told me to call you if I had any more information?"

Daniel had planned to go to BJ's house that morning before the interview with Miss Katz to let her know that she was no longer under suspicion about Carrie's death.

"Are you okay?" he thought she didn't sound right.

"No, sir, I'm not. It's terrible. Just terrible."

He heard her stilted breath and realized she was crying. He sat up in the bed, suddenly completely awake." What happened? Are you in trouble? What is going on?"

She sniffed. "It's Miss Katz. She came to see me last night. And she told me 'bout Carrie."

Daniel groaned again. "BJ, I had planned to see you today and tell you. What did she say? What did you do?"

"I ain't done nothing! What could I do? I didn't kill her. It wasn't me."

"Slow down. Take a deep breath and tell me what happened."

He heard her obediently take in a long breath and let it out. Then she continued, her voice a little stronger. "It's like I told you, Mr. Daniel, she came by the house. As I said, I had been packing to catch a ride to the Alethia House. I told her I had no time to sit and chat, but she said it was important. So I let her in."

"Good. Keep going," prompted Daniel.

"Well, soon as her butt hit the couch, she told me that she done killed my Carrie. She just said it out loud, just like that!"

"I'm sorry, BJ that must have been quite a shock."

"Could have knocked me on my tail with a feather. I wasn't sure I had heard her rightly, so I said, what'd you say? And she said it again. She said, 'I killed Carrie."

"What happened then?"

"I was flabbergasted, like in shock, you know. It was like nuthin' was real. All I said was Why?"

"And what did she say?"

"She said Carrie was a might fussy, which she could be when she got the colic. Miss Katz said she just shook Carrie once to make her quiet down, and then my little girl went to sleep. She didn't know she had hurt Carrie's baby brain until you told her."

Daniel said. "BJ, it's a lot to take in. Do you want me to come over, and we can talk about it?"

"No! You don't get it. I was so mad at the old bitch! I just yelled and yelled at her. I called her an evil woman dressed up as a preacher. I even slapped her silly old face!"

"BJ? What happened then?"

"She didn't hit me back or nuthin'. She just said sorry and walked out of the door."

"Did you follow her?"

He heard the exasperated sigh on the other end. "No, I didn't follow her. I was still in shock. I just sat on the couch and cried. I didn't even go to bed last night; I just sat on that couch crying and thinking. And you know what I thought?"

Daniel had no idea where this conversation was leading. So he remained silent.

"I'll tell you," She didn't seem to notice his lack of response. "I supposed that it wasn't Miss Katz's fault that my angel died."

"What do you mean," he was intrigued.

"No, even though I never laid a hand on my baby, this was still my fault. I used the drugs, and I kept dropping Carrie off with her just because I got tired of being a mommy sometimes. So it's mostly my fault, don't you see, Mr. Daniel."

"I see that you really loved your daughter, and you are realizing that you need help," he offered.

"But Mr. Daniel," she started crying again. "That's not why I called. Yeah, dang it all that happened last night, and mebbe I did some soul searching, but this morning sumpin' horrible happened!'

Daniel began to feel alarmed. "What happened, BJ? Tell me now."

The cries turned to whimpers, and she said, "I went over to Miss Katz's house today to let her know that both of us were in the wrong with Carrie. I knocked and knocked on the door. Her car was in the driveway, so I knew she was home. I thought she might be afraid to open the door on account of the slap last night."

Daniel had a bad feeling and started texting Detective Green to get on down to the Katz home. "Maybe she's just asleep, BJ," he offered. "I am going to head over there now and talk to her. Afterward, maybe you can tell her what you told me."

"No! You can't!" she screamed. "I'm trying to tell you, Mr. Daniel, she's dead!"

"Dead? What do you mean she's dead? How do you know, BJ?"

"She gave me a key once to water her plants when she went out of town. I told her I lost it when she wanted it back, but I really had it. I hate to admit it, but I thought I might go and take some of her pretty things if the money got too tight. Sounds like a dog to say it now. I never did, though!"

"You had a key," he tried to pull the words out of her.

"Yeah, and I opened the door. I went into the bedroom, and she was on her bed. I could tell she was dead cuz I had seen dead bodies."

Daniel thought not to go down that road. "Where are you now, BJ?"

"I'm back at my house. I ran back home and called you up. I thought you might want to know and to tell you I didn't kill her."

"Stay home. I will be at Miss Katz's house in 20 minutes, and so will the police. Just stay home."

He hung up the phone and dialed Jennifer. Filling her in as he quickly dressed, he asked her to ensure Detective Green-met him at the house. She directed him not to enter the home until the police arrived. Then he grabbed a Diet Coke for breakfast and ran to his car.

27

Jennifer

Jennifer spent the day, much like every other day at DHR, assigning cases, providing feedback to her staff on tough calls, and reviewing cases for closure. She ate lunch in her office: a Subway club with pickle chips and coffee. Moving through the routine of her day kept her thoughts of Daniel at bay.

She hadn't heard from him since that morning, and she was both worried for him and relieved. Until they could meet face to face, she would not have to initiate the tough talk that would hurt her probably more than it would him.

At one o'clock, she joined the Secondary Traumatic Stress support group in the conference room on the sixth floor. The group, led by a local counselor, greeted her with warmth and sincerity. She admitted it was her first meeting and asked for some time to observe before jumping in.

Some of the attendees she knew. Danny, the foster care supervisor, had just experienced a child death in his caseload. She was a small child who had been terminally ill with a form of cancer. Her death had been anticipated but nevertheless left an emotional scar. He discussed recently taking up CrossFit to work on some of his pent-up energy.

Katherine Williams, the Adult Service worker, talked about having to remove an eighty-year-old lady from the home she had always known because her physical and mental health had declined. Katherine absorbed all the pain and anxiety of the woman who felt alone and helpless. The counselor discussed ways that Katherine could address her own sadness. A few people that Jennifer did not know related the issues causing them distress, and the group listened and offered encouragement.

"Jennifer?" said the counselor. "Do you want to share with us?"

Jennifer never felt so vulnerable. She didn't tell people about her life, her emotions, and things with which she struggled. But Daniel had been right. The thought of him brought a smile to her face, which she quickly squelched. She had allowed the trauma of losing Candy to overwhelm her.

By assuming guilt and blame for the young woman's choices, Jennifer had almost lost her way. She came to this meeting to learn how to cope better, so she took a deep breath and began.

Without using her name, Jennifer told the group about how she came to be Candy's worker. She talked about the struggles, frustrations, wins, and feelings of success when Candy got into college. Jennifer shared about Candy's death at the hands of her boyfriend and her journey into self-doubt and guilt. Then she shared about Candy's mom and the confession of the broken woman.

As she talked, Jennifer felt herself grow lighter. Although there was still some residual pain, she seemed to understand what Daniel had meant about not letting it bottle up inside.

The counselor nodded as Jennifer talked. When she had finished, he said. "I can see this was a huge loss for you. That tells me how much you care about those you work with. And when they do not succeed, you feel that you failed."

"Yes," she agreed. "I know it's not right, but it is how I feel sometimes."

"There is no right or wrong when it comes to our feelings. Everyone in this room has been or is where you are now." He looked around the room as the other members of the group nodded.

"So, how did you guys stop feeling this? What's the secret?"

The counselor looked to the group, "Alright, I will let you guys answer."

Katherine spoke up. "For me, I had to realize that as long as I work with the vulnerable elderly, I would have to face decisions that would break my heart. What I had to do was realize if this was truly what I wanted to do with my life. When I knew I could answer that it was, then I decided to just accept that I would have some secondary trauma and find ways to take care of my mental health, so it didn't derail me."

"And how did you do that?"

"Well, for me," said Katherine," it meant that every night when I got home, I would go sit on the dock behind my house and watch the lake. Sounds really dumb if I say it out loud. But that is my peaceful place. I can drink a glass of wine, skip rocks if I want, or just sit in my chair and look at the carp, who come to shallow water at dusk to feed. Somehow, just giving my mind 30-45 minutes to decompress allows me to find my center again."

Jennifer nodded. "Okay, I can see how that would help."

A young woman of South Asian appearance spoke up quietly. "I used to have the worst insomnia."

Jennifer recognized her from the In-home unit. "I tortured myself every night wondering if I left a kid in a home unsafe. All night, I would fight those thoughts. Now, I write in a journal. Every night before I go to bed, I jot down what happened that day and how they made me feel. I made sure that I did all I could that day to ensure safety. Once I write everything down, it seems not to hold me hostage anymore. Know what I mean? It's like I got control by putting it on paper."

"I like that idea as well," said Jennifer.

The counselor interjected. "I think the point the group is trying to make is that you have to find what is right for you. What things bring you peace in your life? What brings you joy? Focus on those things and make time for them. By taking care of yourself, you can continue caring for others. And, of course, we are happy to have you anytime you want to join our group."

"I think I would like to keep coming," she said. "At least for a little while longer."

28

Jennifer and Daniel

When 5:00 pm came and went with no word from Daniel, Jennifer really began to worry. She called his cell, and it went straight to voice mail.

"Daniel," she spoke after the tone. "This is Jennifer. I was worried because I hadn't heard from you since your disturbing call this morning. I am going to go home because, like I said earlier this week, the maintenance man promised to fix my air-conditioner., And he missed our last appointment. But please give me a call when you can."

When she reached her apartment, the maintenance man had already come and gone. A note on the door alerted her that the apartment manager had let him in and stayed with him until the job was complete. Although annoyed that they had entered without her knowledge or permission, the cooling breeze she felt upon entrance wiped the annoyance away.

Entering the bedroom, she kicked off her pumps, sighing as her tender feet pressed against the thick carpet. Jennifer shed her dress, changing into a pair of gray jogging pants and an Alabama T-shirt, and began to feel like her normal self. She was just about to throw a Café Steamer into the microwave when she heard a knock at the door.

She looked around to see if the maintenance man had left anything behind as she wasn't expecting company. However, when she reached the door and peeped through the blinds, she saw Daniel. Sweeping her hand through her hair quickly, she opened the door.

"Daniel? What are you doing here? How did you even know where I lived?"

Smiling, he held up a large black handbag.

"My purse? What the hell? Where was it?"

Daniel explained. "I ran by the office to touch base with you and found your office door open and your purse on your desk. I'm unsure how you even drove your car without your keys."

Jennifer looked in amazement. "As for my keys. I had pocketed them earlier when I ran to get a file out of my car. And my car is touch start, so I never even have to touch my keys; otherwise, I might have noticed no purse. I was so caught up in my thoughts when I left that I just walked out of the office. Stupid move, huh?"

"Well, I hope you don't mind, but I knew you couldn't survive without your phone, or I would have just locked up your office for you with your purse there. I called Abernathy's assistant., and she gave me your address. She loves me kind of like a grandson."

Jennifer laughed. "I see. Well, come on in. Sorry to keep you outside. I am just still in denial that I was so careless." She opened the door and ushered him into the living room, grateful she had picked up the scattered clothes earlier.

"Would you like a beer? Or a coke? I also have sweet tea."

"Sweet tea would be great," he said.

Jennifer went into the kitchen to fix the drinks. She turned to see Daniel standing in the doorway, watching her cut into a pan of brownies and transfer them onto a plate.

"What weighed down your mind so much?" he asked.

She decided that that second was not the right time to discuss their need for more professionalism, so she pivoted.

"After the initial call, I was worried about you, and then I heard nothing all day. So I guess that was on my mind when I left."

He took the plate of brownies while she carried the drinks into the living room. Daniel sat on the sofa and took an appreciative sip of the beverage. "I'm glad I was on your mind," he teased.

Jennifer ignored the flirtatious response and asked, "So what happened today?"

Daniel's face lost all of its humor. "Jennifer, you wouldn't believe the day I have had. First, I got a call from BJ early this morning, as I mentioned on the phone."

He gave her the details of his conversation with BJ Ossie and his subsequent trip to meet Detective Green at the Katz home. He told her that Miss Katz committed suicide by taking an entire 90-day supply of her beta-blockers. She was found all dressed in her Sunday best, lying on her freshly made bed. Daniel said that a note had been found on the kitchen table.

"What did it say?" asked Jennifer.

"It read; *I killed an innocent child. I accept my punishment.*"

"Whew! Even in her final words, she seemed so judgmental. And this time, she judged herself," Jennifer remarked.

Daniel just shook his head. "I can't help but feel slightly responsible. I pushed her to tell the truth. I think she suspected all along it was her that killed Carrie. But she hung on to the hope that because Carrie was alive when she left, that something had occurred later that evening."

"No, Daniel. You can't go there."

"I am the one who confronted her with the medical information about Traumatic Brain Injury deaths happening much later than the actual shaking. I burst that bubble of hope for her., And she couldn't accept what she had done. But, Jennifer, I know she did not mean to harm that baby. I think she was tired, frustrated, and at her wit's end."

Most parents who still resort to shaking do so out of their own stress and frustration. Very few parents shake their babies with the intent to kill. Nevertheless, as in the case of Miss Katz, that's exactly what happened. You cannot beat yourself up for telling her the truth."

When Daniel didn't answer, she went on. "And you saved BJ from a possible prison sentence for a crime she never committed. Now, she can get the mental health and substance abuse treatment she needs to get her life back on track. Jason loves his mom, and if she continues to work the program, they can be together again. So, in your search for the truth, you saved two people. Think of it like that."

"I am happy for BJ, and I just hope she takes this opportunity, like you said, to get her life back on track. For her sake and Jason's."

"But it doesn't take away the regret of knowing that Miss Katz committed suicide." Jennifer understood completely. "I could tell you all day that the decision was hers and nothing was your fault. But you and I know that you have to process and come to terms with it."

Daniel nodded. "I know. And I will. I can sort it all out in my head, but in my feelings, I need to do a little more work."

"Well, if it will help, let me tell you about my day."

Jennifer told him all about the support group and how each member stood in a different place in their process of secondary trauma and self-care. "Daniel, it helped, and I want to thank you for telling me about it."

"Will you keep going?" he asked.

Jennifer looked thoughtful. "I think so, at least for a little while. They had some really good ideas. It helped to talk about it out loud. Why don't you come next week with me? Maybe it will help you process Miss Katz's death?"

Daniel smiled. "I would like that. But I don't want to start something I can't finish."

"What do you mean?" she seemed confused.

"Well, I had another reason to talk with you today. I wanted to tell you where I was all afternoon."

"Hmmm, this sounds ominous," replied Jennifer. "Do I want to know? Will the police be calling me?"

Daniel gave a hearty laugh. "I do love your weird sense of humor, Jen."

Jennifer looked at him warily. "Well, out with it. Where were you?"

"I was at a job interview."

"What? What do you mean by a job interview?" The surprise in her voice made it sound shriller than she intended. Lowering her tone, she asked, "What job did you apply for?'

He chuckled. "The Independent Living Coordinator position at the state office. I would coordinate the services for all the youth in foster care over the age of 14, helping them develop the skills and knowledge necessary to make it in the world when they leave foster care. I love working with the teens, you know. This way, I can have some part in making sure that we are providing them with the resources they need to become independent."

He noticed Jennifer's face–her features clouded, but she remained silent.

"Oh, and I didn't apply for it. Perry has been after me for a couple of months to interview for this job. I was on a specialist register but didn't have a reason to interview before this job came up."

Jennifer looked down at her hands, which were clasped in her lap. "I didn't know you were unhappy in our unit."

"Unhappy? Not at all. I have been doing investigations for over ten years. I love it, and I love the unit. And I really love working with you."

Her eyes narrowed. "Then why are you trying to leave.? Are you moving to Montgomery? I don't understand."

Daniel shook his head. "As to moving, they will allow me to remain in the Mobile Office on the sixth floor because my territory would be all of South Alabama."

"Okay. But why leave now?" She knew she was badgering him, but the rejection made her chest hurt.

He looked at her warmly. Then, as he had the day before, he took her hand in his. She did not pull it away this time. "Jennifer, do you really have to ask me that?"

Jennifer felt her heart beat faster. "Apparently, I do."

"Both of us know that there has been a deep connection between us over the past few weeks. At first, I thought it was just attraction because you are unbelievably beautiful."

She hated that she could feel her cheeks redden.

"But I realize that it is more than just attraction. I find myself thinking about you pretty much all the time. I want to get to know you and to be with you. You feel it too, don't you?"

Jennifer met his gaze. "You're not wrong. I feel it, too. But I couldn't allow anything to grow out of it because of our positions."

Daniel added, "Exactly. As long as I worked under you, we could never explore this connection. And I have no desire to be a supervisor. So when this opportunity arose to work as a specialist with teens, I viewed it as a win-win."

Jennifer smiled sweetly, "So, where do we go from here?"

Daniel wrapped his arms around her, pulling her to his chest. "I don't know, but let's do it together wherever we go." Then his lips met hers for a soft kiss and the promise of a new adventure.

Angela McClintock, a Licensed Clinical Social Worker, Certified Trauma Professional, and Child Welfare Consultant, began the Jennifer Riley Series to broadcast the often suppressed voices of families and children in crisis. In telling their stories, Angela wanted to demonstrate that "Hurt people hurt people" and that the villain's identity isn't always so black and white. Similarly, she wanted to dispel the negative portrayal of Social Workers as thoughtless, overworked drones and illuminate the methods and procedures surrounding a fictionalized case. The phenomenon of Secondary Trauma for those who take on the trauma of others is real and experienced widely by Child Welfare Social Workers.

The second book in the series, Grave Justice, was published on April 1, 2025, and continues Jennifer and Daniel's story while they investigate a sexual predator and a drug dealer selling deadly drugs to teens.

Angela lives in Birmingham, Alabama, where she still consults on Child Welfare practice, teaches at a local university, and writes. Her two Corgis, Loki and Odin, keep her grounded.